Are you ready for the journey?

Words Through A Soul
A Fool's Journey

Words Through A Soul
A Fool's Journey

Rajya Lovelife

Words Through A Soul, A Fool's Journey

First edition published in 2023.

Copyright © 2023 Rajya Lovelife. All rights reserved.

Copyright registered with Copyright House, London, U.K. Registration ID: CH218981001

Book cover artwork, 'The Colour Of Creation' Copyright © 2023 Rajya Lovelife
Book cover design Copyright © 2023 Rajya Lovelife

ISBN 978-1-7384194-0-1

No part of this book may be scanned, photocopied, uploaded, reproduced, distributed or transmitted in any form, digital or printed or by any means, including photocopying, recording, or other electronic or mechanical methods, without the prior written permission of the author, with the exception of non-commercial uses permitted by copyright law.
This book does not contain any AI generated texts or art.

The information contained in this book is the author's experience purely for the purpose of self-reflection and helping oneself in one's journey. The author is not responsible for any losses or damages to one's physical, mental or emotional health whatsoever. The reader is responsible for their own spiritual and transformational journeys.

*'Only when we shed the acquired self that
we had become,*

*we become one with the soul,
that's when we become true receivers and
transmitters of divine messages.'*

Contents

Preface i
Introduction vii
Nine Sections Of The Book: xiv
Stage 1: Being A Fool 1
It Is Probably Me 3
Oh, My Love… 4
Being A Fool 6
Stage 2: Pain 9
Isn't It Beautiful? 11
I Know I Have Help 12
Pain 13
Stage 3: Solitude 17
Winter Of Life 19
I Love You Because I Am Love 21
Solitude 22
Stage 4: Awakening 29
Love, But Not Stay In Love 31
The First Flight May Be The Scariest 33
I Do Not Exist Alone 35
My Journey Is Not To A Destination 37
Listen To The Silence 39
You Are Born To Be Who You Are 40

Nectar Of Life 42
Love Within 44
There Is Beauty Everywhere 46
Nature, Oh So 48
Awakening 50

Stage 5: Reflections; In And Out Of Duality 65
Memoirs Of Maggie 67
Wrongs I Did 69
Mountain Of Lie 70
You Once Said 72
Whirlwind Of Thoughts 73
Ho Ima! All I Wanted Was Love 75
Your Contract When You Decide To Become A Parent 77
I Weep For The World 79
Upside-Down World 82
Wasted Day 84
What A Fool I Was! 86
There Is Nothing Such As Wrong 87
Reflections; In And Out Of Duality 88

Stage 6: Coming To The Light, Becoming A Spirit 105
Leaving The Matrix 107
Everything Unfolds With Time 110
Everyone Is Going Through A Challenge 113
Only One Purpose For Everyone 115
I Have Come So Far 117
Be The Spirit That You Are 118
Coming To The Light, Becoming A Spirit 121

Stage 7: The Beginning Of Divine Guidance 133
Phee-Bi's Magic 135
My Angels 139
Shine Your Light 141
The Rise Of The Goddess Consciousness 143
The Beginning Of Divine Guidance 145
Stage 8: Receiving With Absolute Clarity 153
You Must Have It And Lose It 155
Love Is An Energy 157
Love Without 159
One Heart Has All The Love To Heal The Entire Planet 161
Compassion 163
Butterfly Song 166
I'm Proud Of Me 168
Feels Good To Be Home 170
My Union And My Duality 172
The Art Of Surrender 174
Life Is In Surrender 178
The Power Of Growth 179
Rumble's Jenna 180
So Much, You Know Not 186
Receiving With Absolute Clarity 187
Stage 9: Becoming A Powerful Creator 213
I Am No Longer 215
I Am A Powerful Creator 216
Dance With The Universe 218
Becoming A Powerful Creator 220

A Thank You Prayer	227
Index Of Focus	233
Acknowledgements	245
About The Author	248
A Special Dedication	250

Preface

In this section, I am supposed to write, why I am an expert on what I am writing about.

Let me tell you something…I am not a poet, nor a writer, whether I am an expert or not, I leave it to you. I am just a receiver and a transmitter of divine messages. That is why this book is called, *'Words Through A Soul'*, I receive words from The Source of all knowledge through the soul that I am and this is what I am going to share with you. I write as a soul, as a messenger. That is why dear reader, I speak to you, *'A Soul'*, directly because that's how the knowledge was received. I transmit as a soul to a soul in order to awaken what's already within you. I am just a channel for what you seek.

Preface

I see and feel 'energy' in more profound ways than words can explain. Everything is energy. Although I felt it from a very young age, I didn't quite know what I was feeling. It only became clear after I started to have an innerstanding[1] of myself, of this Universe and how it works.

I have been on a conscious journey of going inward for almost 15 years. In the process, I got awakened and started receiving divine guidance…knowledge about healing, about existence, about being a spirit in a human body and how pain propels us to wake up.

Upon awakening, I got to know that it is not just me, but everyone goes through the same journey, we are all mirrors. That is why, it is now my desire to share this knowledge with you, to assist you in your awakening journey to become the true self, to become the powerful creator that you are, to become one with the Universe and go through the adventure of human life with knowing and ease.

---

[1] *Innerstanding – deep knowing from one's experience*

For many years of my life, I was in pain…physically, mentally and emotionally. I was diagnosed with various physical and mental conditions. I was depressed from a very young age, I remember having suicidal thoughts as early as 8-9 years, which carried on into my adulthood. I was not happy, although I didn't know why I was unhappy. I had everything…family, house, material things and comforts that most people would relate to as *'happiness',* but I wasn't happy!

I felt unloved from a very young age, hence, the desire to end my life, but I didn't know why. I had so much pain, but I didn't know why I had them or how to get better. I didn't know how to fix what was wrong in my life and in my body. The diagnoses kept piling up as I got older until the pain became unbearable and I had nowhere else to go. No doctors to fix me, no one to speak to, no one who understood me…I had only one option left…to go inward. That's what I did and that's when things started to shift for me.

For many years of my life, I felt I had nothing to be grateful for. I felt I had nothing to be joyful about, I felt a storm within me that I did not know how to calm. As I

Preface

woke up, I started to see, that all along, the storm had guided me to become the calm that I am today. Now, I am grateful for everything, every single day, there is so much to be grateful for.

Pain acts as a catalyst for us to break through who we have become to get to who we truly are.

That is the journey I went through, from a fool to mastery. These poems signify the journey that everyone goes through.

I started writing poetry at a young age. It was about expressing my deepest emotions. I didn't quite know at the time, that while I was connecting deeply, I was in union with the true self, the soul, the spirit that I am and to *'The Source'* of all beings. I did not know that I was tapping into the realms of higher consciousness until I grew up to pain which had veiled my awareness, my true knowledge for a long time. As I went through the process of unveiling, I started unfolding and connecting to that consciousness, to the true self once again. I am so grateful to my pain now. Without it, I wouldn't be where I am today, healing, learning and growing every single day.

I gave up writing poetry for some years. When I started writing again, I was guided by images as well, so I began to create, which is a process I enjoy, especially these ones included here. The illustrations with dark backgrounds represent the journey from darkness to light, the lotuses symbolise the purity of light that we are.

I was guided to play a part in the human spiritual evolution and so, here I am.

This book is for anybody who enjoys the deeper meaning of life, those who question their existence, those who are consciously waking up, those who want to wake up and those who want to find their true selves. This book is for anybody who wants to leave the darkness behind and step into their true light. I pray that it helps you innerstand[2] your journey, your pain and your experiences in order to wake up, to see with clarity and become the powerful creator that you are.

---

[2] *Innerstand – a standpoint from a deep inner knowing.*

Preface

May this book help you in your transformational journey to shine your light.

Introduction

'Words Through A Soul' is a collection of 55 poems that will take you through a soul journey of emotions. They are accompanied by illustrations made by myself.

A fool's journey is one every human makes, whether you realise it…or not. The stages of the journey are depicted in the style of poetry, as received, which are divided into nine sections in this book…beginning with being attached and weak, then losing love, going through pain and suffering, which triggers awakening, leading to the transformation from naivety to mastery.

Introduction

The journey starts from humanly attachments being interpreted as love which unknowingly weakens one…the racing heart, the feeling of bliss when together, the missing when apart, and the qualm of separation when one loses another, the loneliness, the emptiness, the neediness…the need for somebody to love, to be loved, to be with, indicating the need to be dependent on somebody. Then, going through the pain of separation, which leads to awakening the senses and finding hope. Learning that no matter how great the pain, one has help, there is strength within and there is divine guidance. Realising that pain is needed to grow. Seeing that without darkness, there is no appreciation of true light.

This is followed by the realisation in solitude, that the winter of life is needed to help shed what no longer serves and love is not about the other, but one loves because one is love.

Taking the first flight to heal. Finding the essence and treasures of the journey, learning that it is not about going to a destination, but it is about living the purpose. Discovering that although the path is not easy, there is strength within, there is love within. Seeing the world through the eyes of Source, there is beauty everywhere and lessons from nature.

Going down the road of reflections…realising that the wrongs one does are wrongs done to oneself, not to another. The suffering of going in and out between two worlds during the process of unfoldment, the whirlwind of thoughts, the painful memories, the transitioning in and out between duality and union.

As the journey continues, divine guidance comes through, teaching one to shine the light and create the life one desires. Surrendering to this guidance and the magical transformation happening, the serpent energy awakening and seeing with absolute clarity, what a fool one has been. **Only when one awakens can one see what a fool one has been.** Hence, the knowing that it is needed to be a fool first in order to awaken. This is what everyone's journey is about, from a fool to awakening, from darkness to light, from naivety to mastery.

Finally, releasing all fear, pain and dancing in ecstasy with the Universe, becoming one with the Universe.

Introduction

These are stages that everyone goes through in their lives, knowingly or unknowingly. **Everyone's journey is the same, which is, walking from the outside to the inside. The only differences are the experiences we go through while walking this distance.** The words in this book, are knowledge I have received from The Source, guidance from my Angels and Spirit guides, my Teachers, who have helped me throughout my awakening process. The images are also part of the guidance.

This is also a narration of my own journey…from being a weak and needy person, going through physical, mental and emotional suffering since childhood, followed by the learning that pain is caused by ourselves through our own ignorance and then waking up to true knowledge.

It is my story; I am the fool in it and I am also the awakened one. Some of the poems were written when I identified myself as a human and some, later, as a spirit.

You will notice that this book does not follow the rules of English grammar. It is written as received. In the prose sections, **from Stages 1 to 5**, you will find that it is written in third person, *'she'* is used to describe the fool because I am separating the human from the spirit. This was the time when I identified myself as just a human.

There is another reason why the pronouns *'she'* and *'her'* have been used to describe the person. This is not with reference to my gender, but because *'she'* encompasses *'he'*. Hence, it is a *'she'* and a *'he'* in one word. Within *'her'* is *'he'*.

From Stage 6, *'I'* speak as a soul, narrating the human experience. *'Be The Spirit That You Are'*, indicates the time when I shifted to being a spirit in a human body.

You will also find that it is written in two tenses in the prose sections. For example, excerpts from page 59:

Past tense – "The fool went through this phase in her life. Wanting to be with somebody all her life, even when the relationship served her no more. She thought it was love. She learnt it was attachment."

Present tense – "Many remain together even when the partnership is no longer serving one another. They call it *'love'*. The soul calls it *'attachment'*. In that *'neediness'*, they stay together their entire lives, not knowing that they are only hampering their own growth. You must go on the

Introduction

journey, for, you have growing to do, learnings to carry forward."

The explanation of the verses is in past tense because they are narrations of the fool's journey that were completed, learnings that were already applied.

The knowledge associated with them are written in present tense and there is a reason for that.

The Universe speaks in present tense. There is no past or future. That is why I write all the knowledge that I receive in present tense. For instance, in Stage 2, page 16, instead of writing *'letting go **will** make space for new experiences to come in'*, it is written *'letting go makes space for new experiences to come in.'*

I am grateful to my pain, to my challenges, for initiating me into this journey. My pain was my rite of passage into the queendom of heaven within me, my true home. I am grateful for everything now. I express my gratitude every single day. That's what you will see towards the end of this book, my thank you prayer. I hope you like it. I pray that you may learn to practice gratitude for everything every day after reading this book, especially for your pain and watch your life transform.

Enjoy the journey!

Nine Sections Of The Book:

Stage 1: Being A Fool

{This section is about being in love, being weak and needy}
It Is Probably Me
Oh My Love

Stage 2: Pain

{This section is about the realisation of the beauty of pain}
Isn't It Beautiful?
I know I Have Help

Stage 3: Solitude

{This section is about the need for solitude for inner work}
Winter Of Life
I Love You Because I Am Love

Stage 4: Awakening

{This section is about a conversation between the Acquired Self, the Human (the one that had become) and the True Self, the Soul (the one that is)}

        Love, But Not Stay In Love
        The First Flight May Be The Scariest
        I Do Not Exist Alone
        My Journey Is Not To A Destination
        Listen To The Silence
        You Are Born To Be Who You Are
        Nectar Of Life
        Love Within
        There Is Beauty Everywhere
        Nature, Oh So

Stage 5: Reflections; In And Out Of Duality

{This section is about going down the road of reflections. The suffering of going in and out between two worlds during the process of unfoldment, the transitioning in and out between duality and union}

        Memoirs Of Maggie
        Wrongs I Did
        Mountain Of Lie
        You Once Said
        Whirlwind Of Thoughts

Nine Sections Of The Book

Ho Ima! All I Wanted Was Love
Your Contract When You Decide To Become A Parent
I Weep For The World
Upside-Down World
Wasted Day
What A Fool I was!
There Is Nothing Such As Wrong

Stage 6: Coming To The Light, Becoming A Spirit

{This section is about leaving the illusionary world to become the spirit that you are}

Leaving The Matrix
Everything Unfolds With Time
Everyone Is Going Through A Challenge
Only One Purpose For Everyone
I Have Come So Far
Be The Spirit That You Are

Stage 7: The Beginning Of Divine Guidance

{This section is about receiving divine guidance to shine your light}

Phee-Bi's Magic
My Angels
Shine Your Light
The Rise Of The Goddess Consciousness

Stage 8: Receiving With Absolute Clarity

{This section is about living with clarity, about doing everything from a place of knowing}

You Must Have It And Lose It
Love Is An Energy
Love Without
One Heart Has All The Love To Heal The Entire Planet
Compassion
Butterfly Song
I'm Proud Of Me
Feels Good To Be Home
My Union And My Duality
The Art Of Surrender
Life Is In Surrender
The Power Of Growth
Rumble's Jenna
So Much, You Know Not

Nine Sections Of The Book

Stage 9: Becoming A Powerful Creator

{This section is about becoming who you are, about being a spirit on a magical journey to become one with the divine that you are}

I Am No Longer
I Am A Powerful Creator
Dance With The Universe

Stage 1: Being A Fool

Stage 1: Being A Fool

It Is Probably Me

My head is spinning
My heart is racing

Is it you? Or is it me?
It is probably me

Feels like you've taken over my life
Feels like I am caught in a whirlwind
Feels like it is all too fast

Feels like I want to get out of it
Feels like I am paralysed
Feels like I am panicking

My head is spinning
My heart is racing
Is it you? Or is it me?
It is probably me

Stage 1: Being A Fool

Oh, My Love…

Oh, my Love, I miss you so…

When will my heart stop aching for you?
Feel like I will wither away without you.

Wish you were here with me,
Wish I could say, 'come see me'.

But far away you are,
Into the wide blue yonder you are.

Oh, my Love, I love you so…

How I wish I could tell you,
How much I long for you.

To be together,
Forever in every weather.

But the qualm of separation,

Words Through A Soul

Leaves me with frustration.

Oh, my Love, I want you so…

The love in my heart shall never die,
This I confess to you I never lie.

Stained by the colours of love,
I pray to the Gods above.

To take away my loneliness,
To take away my emptiness.

Stage 1:
Being A Fool

The journey starts with humanly attachments being interpreted as *'love'*.

The fool was young and she thought she was in love, she experienced the spinning head, the racing heart and those sensations completely took her over for a while. Made her feel like she was paralysed or caught in a whirlwind, beyond her control. Made her feel like there was nothing else or no one else in the world apart from her love, just completely absorbed in it. This is the feeling described in the first poem, '*It Is Probably Me*'.

This poem emphasises on the silliness of being a fool. At the same time, the inner knowing somewhere deep within. Although she wasn't listening yet, somehow knowing that whatever was happening, was probably within herself and not because of another. The fool was beginning to question.

'Is it you? Or is it me?
It is probably me'

'Oh, My Love' is about the missing when apart and the aching heart when one loses another, the loneliness, the emptiness…whether through death or physical separation.

'But far away you are,
Into the wide blue yonder you are.'

'Stained by the colours of love,
I pray to the Gods above.

To take away my loneliness,
To take away my emptiness.'

The pain of separation, also the beginning of pain in the fool's journey. I identified her as a fool at this point because she was not yet aware of her humanness. **That what she thought was love, was only attachment.** That what she thought was love and missing, only made her weak because by feeling empty without the other, she had given her power away to another.

In loving someone, you must have no expectation of time or space. Therefore, if one is lonely or empty because of the loss of another, it can only mean that it was not love, it was *'attachment'*, the *'need'* to be with somebody. If you truly love somebody and lose her through the loss of her physical body, you know that she always exists in spirit. Because we are spirits in a temporary vehicle called the human.

Stage 2: Pain

Stage 2: Pain

Isn't It Beautiful?

Isn't it beautiful?
The feelings of love, oh so wonderful!

Isn't it beautiful?
The desires of love, oh so blissful!

Isn't it beautiful?
The excitement of longingness, oh so dream-full!

Isn't it beautiful?
The bittersweet of senses, oh so painful!

Isn't it beautiful?
The pain of separation, oh so hopeful!

Stage 2: Pain

I Know I Have Help

Pain in my heart, I have to let you go.
Longing in my heart, I have to watch you go.
Do I know I have help?

How do I stop this pain, I have?
How do I stop this love, I have?
Do I know I have help?

I want just a little easier.
I want just a little lighter.
I know I have help.

I know I am strong, although I seem weak.
I know I am well, although I seem bleak.
I know I have help.

Pain in my heart, I let you go.
Longing in my heart, I watch you go.
I know I have help.

Stage 2

Pain

'*Isn't it beautiful?*'

This poem talks about the pain of separation. The reason why the adjective '*beautiful*' is used for pain, is to highlight the fact that pain is beautiful, if you know that it is needed for your growth. To experience true light, you must first experience darkness. **Pain is the much-needed darkness. It is the key that unlocks the door to allow light in.**

In this poem, the fool was still experiencing the longingness, the bitterness of separation, but at the same time the sweetness of the feelings of love, hence, '*bittersweet*'. She was also beginning to be hopeful although she was still in pain... '*the pain of separation oh so hopeful*'.

Stage 2: Pain

The word *'hopeful'* is used although she was in pain, to bring your awareness to the fact that you may go through pain, but you must not allow yourself to remain in misery. You may be sad, lonely, grieve or mourn when you lose someone, but when you realise that pain is vital for your growth, you can become hopeful. Hope is the next step up, to come out of misery. It is hope that gives you the promise, that there is light in the distance. It is hope that gives you the courage to take that step. **One cannot jump from total darkness to light in an instance.** It is like moving from black to white. There are many transitional greys in between. You may not see them with your naked eyes, but they are there. You must go through each shade, in order to transition from pain to ecstasy.

Thus, feeling hopeful was a transitional phase for the fool.
    Although she was still going through pain, she was starting to realise that she had help from the divine realm… *'I Know I Have Help'*.
    Initially she did not know that she had help, *'do I know I have help?'* She had to learn to let go, enforced by life's situation, to learn this lesson.

'Pain in my heart, I have to let you go.'

Somehow deep inside, she believed she had help. So, she started to ask… *'I want just a little easier'*…this was her declaration to the Universe, to help her release her heaviness, to feel just a little lighter.

She was now beginning to tune in to her inner knowing… *'I know I am strong, although I seem weak.'* She found comfort in the knowing that she had help. She was opening herself to the willingness to learn to let go.

'Pain in my heart, I let you go.
Longing in my heart, I watch you go.
I know I have help.'

No matter how much suffering you are experiencing, when you lose somebody, you must let go. No matter how much *'in love'* you think you are, if it is the time to let go, you must let go. For, it is in the letting go, that you receive new energies. Many people struggle to let go because they are unable to trust that they have help, that the Universe is there for them, that something better is unfolding for them. So, they hold on, to memories, to things, to people, to situations and in that, you choose to stay in pain and

Stage 2: Pain

not heal. **Letting go makes space for new experiences to come in.** It is all energy. If you hold on, you are blocking up that space. So, let go and allow new energies to come into your life.

Stage 3: Solitude

Stage 3: Solitude

Winter Of Life

Winter of life comes and goes,
Just the way seasons do.

Winter of life...
    ...helps shed who no longer serves.
    ...helps preserve energy.
    ...teaches you strength in solitude.
    ...teaches you to fight your fears.

Without the winter of life, there is no appreciation of spring.
Without the pains of life, there is no appreciation of true joy.
Without darkness, there is no appreciation of light.
Without death, there is no appreciation of new life.

Winter of life...
    ...is needed to grow.
    ...is perfect for unfoldment.
    ...teaches you there's always a promise.

Stage 3: Solitude

…teaches you to climb the summit of life.

Winter of life comes and goes,
Just the way seasons do.

I Love You Because I Am Love

I love you, for who I am.
I love you, for what I am.

I love you, not because of who you are,
I love you, not because of what you are,

I love you, not so you love me back,
I love you, not so you want me back,

It is not about you, this love,
It is about me, this love,

I am happy you are not the perfect one,
I am happy you are not the chosen one,

This love I have, is who I am.
This love I have, is what I am.

I love you because I am love.

Stage 3
Solitude

Solitude is vital for the soul's journey.

The fool had now entered the journey of pain and solitude. Her pain so intense had given rise to the questions…*'why me?'*…*'why am I suffering?'* She had questioned and she had agreed to take her time to find the answers in solitude.

Winter of life comes and goes…everything changes, nothing remains the same. The seasons of life…pain may come, but pain does not have to stay, you must let it go. **Life must continue to change just the way seasons do.**

Winter may seem bare, bleak and harsh, but it signifies solitude perfectly.

She had to go through harshness, for life to teach her, how to shed those layers. To let go of those people whom she was clinging on to, those who no longer served in her journey. Yes, she had to learn it the hard way because she wasn't willing to do it the easy way. She wasn't listening until pain hit her. In solitude, she learnt that she was spending so much energy trying to make everything work, when it wasn't working, trying to be happy when she wasn't, trying to change others, trying to hold on to every situation in her life. After she learnt to let go, she realised how much energy she was beginning to preserve. Energy, which she could now use for her own healing journey. She started to find the strength in solitude. She started to get stronger. She started to learn to fight her fears.

The fool started to realise that without challenges, there could be no appreciation of opportunities. Without darkness, there would be no appreciation of light. She did not see this when she was in the dark. She realised this only as she began to come out of her own darkness, that's when she began to see the true meaning of light.

Stage 3: Solitude

She saw in nature how everything died down in the winter and they all came back to life in spring. This became her knowing…that harsh winter was required, for those plants to save their energy, so that they can burst back to life. Just the same way as she was doing for her journey inward, for her unfoldment, to become who she really was. There was a promise, she started to see, there was life after pain, and she was beginning to know that she could climb the summit of her life.

Solitude is required for inner work. Just as winter is needed for spring…certain seeds, plants in nature must go through the incubation period of winter to shoot out in spring. Just as a child must go through the period of nine months inside the mother's womb, you must go through solitude for some time in darkness in order to grow.

You may wonder…isn't solitude the same as loneliness? What is the difference between the two?…in both cases, you are on your own? The difference is, loneliness is dictated by someone else or some situation outside of you, hence, you lose your power because you are not in control. Solitude is your choice. You are in control.

Loneliness is emptiness. **Solitude is choosing to quiet the mind.** In loneliness, you weep because you are far away from the soul. **In solitude, you start to hear the whispers of the soul.**

In solitude, the fool began to see that love was not about the other, but one loves because one is love.

She also started to see the blessing in disguise when she lost her lover. At first, she cried that he was not the perfect one, then, she started to become grateful as she saw the blessing. Had she remained with him; she would've never got this opportunity for solitude. Thus, she learnt to become grateful that he was not the chosen one. This learning started to change her. She started to be kind to herself. She started to learn that she loves because she is love. *'I Love You Because I Am Love'*.

Many people love another in the expectation to be loved back. Many people love and tell each other why they love, what it is about the other that makes them happy. Lay conditional rules... *'I love him because he is so clever, he is doing so well in his life'* or *'I love her because she is so beautiful'*.

Stage 3: Solitude

Would you continue to love him, if he lost all his material possessions? Could you love her, if she lost her external beauty?

When you expect love from another because you are giving love to that person, when you expect a return, you are bound to be disappointed at some point. Because most times, life turns out different from what you expect when you live by default.

The thing about expectation is that it is an energy where you have given your power away to another. You have sent out a little ball of energy through your desire of expectation, a piece of your love, a piece of yourself and if it is met, then there is balance. The little ball of energy that you sent out has returned to you through another and therefore, you are happy. That's how energy works. Everything that goes must come back.

However, when you do not receive what you expect, you remain incomplete. Then, you start to react. You may get upset or act out as *'anger'* towards your partner or friend. You start to build up feelings of rejection inside yourself, jumping to conclusions such as... *'She has not done it because she does not love me anymore'*, etc. The little ball of energy you sent out has not returned.

Can you see how fragmented you can become when you have so many unmet expectations? Pieces of you flying everywhere.

When you love because you are love, you have no expectations. You do it because that's who you are. So, you have not sent out a piece of yourself towards another, the love is never given away to somebody. It stays within you. **You remain complete.** In which case, whether a person remains in your life or not, whether another does anything for you or not, it makes no difference to your love, to your joy because you are a whole.

'This love I have, is who I am.
This love I have, is what I am.'

Stage 3: Solitude

Stage 4: Awakening

Stage 4: Awakening

Love, But Not Stay In Love

You must leave because you took the wrong step.
You must change because you want to grow.

You took a wrong turn on your journey,
Wouldn't you turn around?
Wouldn't you move towards the right direction that can take you to where you want to go?

You stay in the same place for years,
Even when you know you have taken the wrong turn,
You call it "love".

I call it "attachment".
I call it "fear".
I call it "weakness".

The important thing is the turning,
The important thing is your realisation,
The important thing is your journey.

Stage 4: Awakening

Some may say, you have used them.
Some may say, you are heartless.
Some may say, you are ambitious.

But you know who you are,
You know what's important.

You may love, but not stay in love,
For love is pure and needs no return,
For staying in love becomes needy.

Why stay in love with the past?
Why live your past every single day?
Love, but not stay in love with the past.

The First Flight May Be The Scariest

The first flight may be the scariest but do it anyway.
The first step may be the hardest but take it anyway.
The first move towards self-love may feel effortful but try it anyway.
The first stride towards self-realisation may seem strenuous but start it anyway.
The first journey towards self-healing may seem challenging but go on it anyway.

---

[3] *Art Title: First Flight Of The Phoenix*

Stage 4: Awakening

You have to do it one day or the other.

No one can escape this.

If you don't, it knocks harder.
If you don't, it gets louder.
The sooner you realise, the sooner you learn.
The sooner you learn, the sooner you grow.
The sooner you grow, the sooner you heal.

I Do Not Exist Alone

I cannot exist alone
I only exist because of the flow

I cease to exist without the flow
If I do not exist, does my body exist?

I only exist in relation to you all
I only exist because of your guidance

I continue to learn
I continue to be guided

For, I do not exist alone

Stage 4: Awakening

4

---

[4] *Art Title: The Journey.*

[Elements in the artwork – letting go (depicted by the floating balloons); holding on (depicted by the balloons tied to the trees); guidance available (depicted by the moon); prosperity, creativity (depicted by the rabbits); heading towards the light (depicted by the path); abundance (depicted by the trees, plants, flowers, flower of life); surprises (depicted by the gift boxes)]

My Journey Is Not To A Destination

My journey is taking me on my path.
My journey is living my purpose.
My journey is not to a destination.

My journey is perfect,
Even when I face challenges.
For, I know they are signs guiding me towards the right direction,
That's how I know my journey is perfect.

My journey is abundant,
Even when I have nothing.
For, I know this is exactly what I created and
I can create whatever I want,
That's how I know my journey is abundant.

My journey is healing,
Even when I have pain.
For, I know it is conditional and I can release it,
That's how I know my journey is healing.

Stage 4: Awakening

My journey is full of surprises,
Even when I am lost.
For, I know I can trust, and everything is always working out,
That's how I know my journey is full of surprises.

My journey is love and only love,
Even when I have no one to love.
For, I know this is the solitude I need to embrace, to find love within,
That's how I know my journey is love and only love.

My journey is taking me on my path.
My journey is living my purpose.
My journey is not to a destination.

Listen To The Silence

Learn to be still
Away from the noise

It may terrify you at first
But stick with it

Learn to breathe
The calm of nature

It may frighten you at first
But stick with it

Only when you learn to be still
Can you teach your children to be still

Only when you learn to breathe
Can you master your mind and body

Only in the stillness of silence
Can you truly find you

Stage 4: Awakening

You Are Born To Be Who You Are

You are born to be wild and free,
You are born to thrive and blossom,
You are born to nurture and grow.

On an ever changing, constantly growing journey,
Try you must, of everything, so you lead a life of no regrets,
Be the one, to listen to the whispers of the soul.

Who you are, must be what you are,
Life takes you there, allow you must,
You are born to be who you are.

[5] *Art Title: Wild And Free ~ The Fearless Goddess*

Stage 4: Awakening

6

Nectar Of Life

She said, "stay with me and drink my nectar all your life."
He replied, "go, I must, for, I have growing to do, experiences to learn from and memories to lock into the soul, to carry forward."

A soul is free,
A soul must be free,
For, freedom is true existence.

---

[6] *Art Title: Nectar Of Life*

No matter how strong the attachment,
Letting go is freeing.

No matter how dark it seems,
There's always light.

No matter how lost you feel,
There's always guidance.

No matter how muddy the waters,
Choose to blossom with all your purity,
just like the lotus.
No matter how challenging the darkness,
Choose to be playful and drink the nectar of life with ease, just like the hummingbird.
Choose to be, who you really want to become, who you really are.

Stage 4: Awakening

Love Within

Weak on the outside, strong within.
Shy on the outside, courageous within.
Anxious on the outside, confident within.
Naïve on the outside, knowing within.
Confused on the outside, clarity within.

Chaos on the outside, calm within.
Worry on the outside, peace within.
Insanity on the outside, balance within.
Lack on the outside, abundant within.
Difficult on the outside, ease within.

Miserable on the outside, joyful within.
Suffering on the outside, blessing within.
Guilt on the outside, virtue within.
Neglect on the outside, appreciation within.
Dishonour on the outside, respect within.

Control on the outside, surrender within.
Sparing on the outside, generous within.

Grudging on the outside, willing within.
Defective on the outside, precious within.
Inferior on the outside, worthy within.

Envy on the outside, kindness within.
Sadness on the outside, faith within.
Anger on the outside, eager within.
Despise on the outside, cheer within.
Fear on the outside, love within.

Stage 4: Awakening

There Is Beauty Everywhere

There is beauty everywhere.
There is joy everywhere.
There is love everywhere.

It is your choice, whether you choose to see the beauty around or the dirt and the unpleasantness.
It is your choice, whether you see joy or disappointment and frustration.
It is your choice, whether you feel love or hatred and jealousy.
It is your choice, whether you wallow in pain or see the inner strength that is emerging.
It is your choice, whether you fill yourself with emotions that lift you up or take you down.

You always have a choice.
You just have to look.
You just have to see.

It is your choice, whether you continue to live a painful yesterday or build a happier tomorrow.
It is your choice, whether you remain the "*same old you*" or evolve to the *"real you"*.
It is your choice, whether you line up to divine guidance or remain ignorant.
It is your choice, whether you stay stuck or grow.
It is your choice, whether you start today or never start.

You always have a choice.
You just have to look.
You just have to see.

There is beauty everywhere.
There is joy everywhere.
There is love everywhere.

Stage 4: Awakening

Nature, Oh So

Nature, oh so beautiful
Nature, oh so graceful
Nature, oh so inspiring
Nature, oh the greatest artist
Nature, oh the incredible teacher

Nature, oh so loving
Nature, oh so nurturing
Nature, oh so sacred
Nature, oh so intense
Nature, oh so grounding

Nature, oh so calming
Nature, oh so healing
Nature, oh so invigorating
Nature, oh so purifying
Nature, oh so powerful

[7] *Art Title: We Are Nature*

Stage 4

Awakening

The fool had contemplated in solitude, taken the time to go inward and this had triggered her senses to awaken.

'Love, But Not Stay In Love' is a conversation between **the Acquired Self, The Human (the one that had become) and the True Self, The Soul (the one that is).** The fool called it *'love'*, I, as a soul, call it *'attachment'*.

The fool had started to see that she took the wrong step and until she became aware, she kept going deeper and deeper into the dark. As soon as she realised it, she began to see that she must change her course in order to go towards the right direction. The fool was waking up.

Many people think they are in love and stay together for a long time, even when there is no joy left in each other's company. When you realise this, you must be willing to change because you took the wrong turn in your life.

'You took a wrong turn on your journey,
Wouldn't you turn around?
Wouldn't you move towards the right direction
that can take you to where you want to go?'

If you are heading towards a destination and you keep going in the wrong direction, are you ever going to arrive at the desired place? The answer is 'No'. Hence, as soon as you realise this, you must move towards the right direction. **The realisation is important because without it you can never make the move.**

'The important thing is the turning,
The important thing is your realisation,
The important thing is your journey.'

Many people stay together, for, they fear what others might say.

'Some may say, you have used them.
Some may say, you are heartless.
Some may say, you are ambitious.'

Stage 4: Awakening

In that, you live for the society, for the family, for the others, not for yourself. That is nothing but *'fear'* and *'weakness'*.

'But you know who you are,'

Your journey is important to you. You know where you want to go. You know what you want to be. **You must not allow a wrong turn to keep you in the wrong place for your entire life.**

If it is pure love, it is all within you. You love because you are love. You love because that's who you are. You never give away any part of you, you remain complete. If it is pure love, you love without any expectation. If you stay because you are weak and you call it *'in love'*, then you are being needy, it is not love.

Calling it love and staying in it, even when there is no joy, is living in the past, because you are not moving on. You are love, but you do not have to live your past every single day.

'Why stay in love with the past?
Why live your past every single day?

Love, but not stay in love with the past.'

This also points towards the time of realisation for the fool to start working on becoming the love that she is, on being pure love.

'The First Flight May Be The Scariest'…the fool had taken the first step to self-love, self-realisation, self-healing.

The first step is always the hardest in life for humans. When you learn to walk as a child, the first step may seem effortful, the scariest one to take, but you try it anyway because that's what your body is guiding you towards.

When you haven't learnt how to be aware, it may seem tiring to start paying attention to everything. When you haven't learnt how to be love, how to heal yourself, they may all seem challenging at first, but listen to the guidance of life and go on it anyway because you have to do it one day or the other.

'No one can escape this.'

If you do not listen, that's fine too. It only gets louder until you listen because it is that part of you which needs healing, and the soul is guiding you towards that.

The sooner you realise it, the quicker you learn to grow and heal.

'I Do Not Exist Alone' was the beginning of the realisation by the fool that she was not just physical, that there was a flow of energy, without which, the physical body would cease to exist. It was also the time of learning that even in solitude, there is guidance available and that she was not alone.

You are not just a physical body. You are not a human with a soul. **You are an *'Energy Being'* in a temporary vehicle called the human body.** Life force energy flows to you and through you, without which the body perishes.

You are never alone. There is always guidance available for everybody. All you have to do is start your journey inward to listen to that guidance. All you do is ask and it is given. You do not exist alone, even in solitude.

'My Journey Is Not To A Destination' is about learning to trust the journey. Trusting the process, trusting that there

is guidance, trusting that everything is working out, no matter what.

The fool was willing to go all the way, she was beginning to open to surprises, learning to let go of control. Beginning to see that the journey was not about arriving at a destination, but it was about living her purpose.

Many people identify the word *'perfect'* to having no blemishes, no cracks, no pain, no suffering, **but perfection is knowing that challenges are perfect for your journey.** Therefore, when you encounter pain, it is perfect, for, they are signs guiding you towards the right direction. When you feel gratitude towards your pain for this very reason, you release the pain and heal. When you start to listen to your inner guidance, you can create whatever you want for your greater good.

In solitude, she found the true love that was within her. Not love from another, not love for another, not love for herself, but just love.

'My journey is love and only love,

Even when I have no one to love.
For, I know this is the solitude I need to embrace, to find love within,
That's how I know my journey is love and only love.'

When you let go of all fears, you start to receive the guidance that is available for you. When you let go of all control, you start to see the surprises that life has to offer, opening doors for you along the path. Trust the process and know that life is abundant. Know that the journey is only love.

The fool was appreciating her journey and her solitude now. She was becoming aware of the divine guidance that was coming through. Although it was frightening at first, she kept going, guided by her inner voice.

As the fool was awakening, she recognised how noisy her mind used to be, how noisy the world was.

An unconscious life is full of noise, constantly doing, busy with actions all the time, too much information that clog the mind. Learn to be still, away from the noise...*'Listen*

To The Silence'…only then can you master your mind and body.

In your solitude, it may seem lonely at first, it may seem scary at first, but keep going, for, only in the stillness of silence can you truly find yourself.

Why is it important to find yourself? **Because that is the journey everyone has to do, travel from the outside to the inside. For, only when you find the true self, do you find true peace, true love, true joy.** Only when you learn this, can you teach your children and be an example to others around you. That is why, only when you find yourself, can you be of true service to yourself, to humankind, to the planet and to the entire Universe.

'You Are Born To Be Who You Are'…many humans become who they are not. Some become a wife, some become a mother, some become a manager, a lawyer, some become dependent, some become a victim, some become terrified…they are not who they are.

You are born to be wild and free, for, only when you are free can you thrive and blossom. Freedom does not mean that you have to remain on your own throughout your life or be irresponsible. Freedom means being with others who see you for who you are and allow you to be who you truly are, which means, it must be an ever-evolving relationship, embracing that change for the true unfoldment of all. Freedom means allowing your children to be who they are, not controlling them through your own desires and suffocating them with your attachment, what you call *'love'*. Freedom means trust. Freedom means respecting each other's boundaries and being considerate. **Freedom means taking responsibility for yourself.** Only then can you truly nurture and grow, only then can you allow others to grow.

Who you are is guided by the soul, you must learn to listen to the whispers. Any guidance you receive, you must try it out. It may not work out well every time you try something new, go somewhere new, but only when you try can you know.

'Try you must, of everything, so you lead a life of no regrets,'
You do not want a day to come in your life, when you say, *'I wish I had done that'*.

You must continue to evolve, continue to grow on a constantly changing journey. You must allow life to take you there. All you have to do, is have the desire to be who you are, to become what you are. Life brings you the opportunities. **What you are, is not about becoming something on the outside, it is about allowing yourself to shed the outer layers of what you are not.**

'Who you are, must be what you are,
Life takes you there, allow you must,
You are born to be who you are.'

'Nectar Of Life'
'She said, "stay with me and drink my nectar all your life".'
The fool went through this phase in her life. Wanting to be with somebody all her life, even when the relationship served her no more. She thought it was love. She learnt it was attachment.

Many remain together even when the partnership is no longer serving one another. They call it *'love'*. The soul calls it *'attachment'*. In that *'neediness'*, they stay together their entire lives, not knowing that they are only hampering their own growth. **You must go on the journey, for, you have growing to do, learnings to carry forward.**

'He replied, "go, I must, for, I have growing to do, experiences to learn from and memories to lock into the soul, to carry forward".'

All souls long to be free, for, a spirit is free. The soul is not bound by any rules, any time, any limitations. **Letting go is freeing.**

No matter how lost you feel, no matter how dark it seems, *'Choose to blossom with all your purity, just like the lotus'*. No matter how muddy the water, a lotus always pops its head up and blossoms in all its purity. That's what you must choose, to blossom, to unfold, to grow, no matter how much pain, how much darkness you have gone through, choose to seek the light. **When you choose, you are willing, you are allowing life to lead you, to become who you really are.**

'No matter how challenging the darkness,
Choose to be playful and drink the nectar of life with ease,
just like the hummingbird.

Choose to be, who you really want to become, who you really are.'

As the fool continued to expand, she began to see that she had everything inside of her. As she let go of what was on the outside, she found what was inside.

'Confused on the outside, clarity within.'

You are a complete package as you are. You may seem weak on the outside, but you have strength within. You may seem chaotic on the outside, but you have all the calm within. You may be fearful on the outside... fear of diseases, fear of death, fear of uncertainty, but fear only takes control when you do not connect to the love within. When you are love, you have the love of the divine, for, when you are love, you connect to the entire universe, to The Source of all. When you know this, you are strong and secured, there is no place for fear. You have *'Love Within'*.

The fool was beginning to realise, there was everything within...knowing, clarity, balance, abundance, ease, joy,

Stage 4: Awakening

appreciation, blessing, faith, miracle. She also realised that everything existed everywhere at the same time…beauty or unpleasantness, joy or disappointment, love or hatred. All she had to do was to make a choice, which one she wanted to see, in anybody, in any situation.

When you feel the love within, you see that *'There Is Beauty Everywhere'* because you see through the eyes of love, the eyes of Source. Everything exists at all times…love or hatred, pain or strength, whether you live in the past, remain the same old you, or evolve to the real you…it is your choice how you want your life to be. You always have a choice.

'It is your choice, whether you continue to live yesterday or build a happier tomorrow.

It is your choice, whether you remain the "same old you" or evolve to the "real you".'

The fool spent more time in solitude, in nature, being one with nature. She began to feel the true connection. She began to be tremendously inspired by nature. She began to see the essence of nature, the pure beauty, every layer of colour, the blending to perfection like an artists' masterpiece. She began to feel the lessons, the knowledge and the healing power of Mother Nature. She began to truly connect with creation.

When you awaken the love within, you become one with nature. You begin to harness the power of *'Nature, Oh So'* beautiful. Nature is the greatest artist. She is an incredible teacher, a healer like no one. **She is the Divine Mother who loves and nurtures all beings.** She cleanses you, purifies you, invigorates you, grounds you. She is, oh so powerful.

Stage 4: Awakening

When you learn to truly become one with nature, you learn the true essence of your own life, every life, every existence. You are nature.

Stage 5: Reflections; In And Out Of Duality

Stage 5: Reflections; In And Out Of Duality

Memoirs Of Maggie

She annoyed me one morning by barking out loud at
five, it was midnight for me!
I jumped out of bed, grumpily...

Sleepily, I looked out of the window,
And what a magnificent scene, I saw.
Dear God! did it melt my heart...

The sun was just breaking out,
Soft light filtering through the trees,
The mist from the river beyond,
The farmer's cows grazing lazily,
The pink horse chestnut blossoms beautifully lit...

It was a moment of such joy for my eyes and my heart,
Such splendour that only mother nature can unravel.
She is the greatest artist.

A lesson I learnt from that morning...

Stage 5: Reflections; In And Out Of Duality

"No matter how annoying an experience in life,
Be open to see what it is waking you up to,
What unexpected beauty, it is showing you.
So, do not focus on the annoyance at life,
But look around and be open to see what it is trying to show you,
Something beautiful you do not want to miss.
The annoyance is just an alarm, so that you don't miss it."

She was barking at the cows.
Had I just shushed her and not looked out of the window,
I would have missed this breath-taking scene.

Such a beautiful lesson!
I am so very grateful to Maggie, my baby girl.
Love always.

Wrongs I Did

Wrongs I did, were wrongs done to myself.

Wrongs I did, were wrongs that flourished from fear.

Wrongs I did, were wrongs that stemmed from ignorance.

Wrongs I did, were wrongs that grew from darkness.

Wrongs I did, were wrongs that sprung from lack.

Wrongs I did, were wrongs that rose from rejection.

Wrongs I did, were wrongs that came from needing love.

Stage 5: Reflections; In And Out Of Duality

Mountain Of Lie

A mountain of lie,
It takes a long time to chisel.

It gets bigger and bigger,
Until you learn what you must.

How to stay where you don't want to be, learn from me!
How to stay doing what you don't want to do, learn from me!

I stayed for so long, doing things I don't want to do.
I stayed for so long, being in places I don't want to be.
I scare myself when I look back.

Why did I do such a thing?
Did I not love myself?
Did I do it knowingly?

It was ignorance.
It was neediness.

It was weakness.
It was self-doubt.
It was fear.

I forgive myself,
For, that was the only way I could learn,
For, that was the only way I could shed the old ignorant me.
For, that was the only way I could come to the light.
For, that was the only way I could become strong.

I trusted.
I remained calm.
I focussed on my journey.
I chiselled the mountain a little by little.
For, I learnt, that mistakes are only steppingstones towards true knowledge.

Are you building a mountain of lie?

Stage 5: Reflections; In And Out Of Duality

You Once Said

You once said, you loved me.
Did you know what love is?

You once said, you wanted to be with me.
Did you know what want is?

You once said, you appreciated me.
Did you know what appreciation is?

You once said, you respected me.
Did you know what respect is?

You once said, you were grateful for me.
Did you know what gratitude is?

Whirlwind Of Thoughts

Whirlwind of thoughts,
Where do they come from?

Whirlwind of thoughts,
They make me weary.

Whirlwind of thoughts,
They make me fearful.

Whirlwind of thoughts,
They make me angry.

Whirlwind of thoughts,
They make me anxious.

Whirlwind of thoughts,
They make me react.

Whirlwind of thoughts,
They make me shiver.

Stage 5: Reflections; In And Out Of Duality

Whirlwind of thoughts,
They make me suffer.

Whirlwind of thoughts,
I can't seem to stop.

Ho Ima![8] *All I Wanted Was Love*

Ho Ima! I wished you had more time for me,
For, you were busy with no time for yourself.

Ho Ima! I wished you could see my heart,
For, you were engrossed in fighting your own pain.

Ho Ima! I wished you could feel my trouble,
For, you were battling your own struggle.

Ho Ima! I wished you could look at my cuts,
For, you were stabbed in your own heart.

Ho Ima! I wished we had more time,
For, you were kept in your own darkness.

Ho Ima! I wished it was easier for us,
For, I know you wished life was a piece of cake.

---

[8] *"Ho" is a word used for calling out to somebody and "Ima" means mother in Manipuri (Meiteilon), the author's native language.*

Stage 5: Reflections; In And Out Of Duality

Ho Ima! All I wanted was love,
Ho Ima! All you wanted was love.

Your Contract When You Decide To Become A Parent

The day you decide to become a parent,
You sign a contract with yourself to reinvent yourself,
From that moment on,
Every move you make, every word you use,
Every emotion you generate, everything you do,
You are going to create another just like you.

You want your child to be strong, you be.
You want your child to be independent, you be.
You want your child to be responsible, you be.
You want your child to be creative, you be.
You want your child to be healthy, you be.
You want your child to be respectful, you be.
You want your child to be joyful, you be.
You want your child to be kind, you be.
You want your child to be generous, you be.
You want your child to be gracious, you be.
You want your child to be compassionate, you be.

Stage 5: Reflections; In And Out Of Duality

Your child is not a child, she is a soul.

You, as a mother, simply house her for nine months.

You, as a mother, are simply there to help her until she is ready.

But you get attached by giving it a label.

Let go when she is able.

This is by design, as nature intended it to be.

I Weep For The World

I weep for the world, building problem over problem.

Depending on all things external,
Running from one way to another,
Delaying their ascension,
Taking them further away from themselves,
Looking for that answer, which already exists within them.

I weep for the world, making it denser and denser.

Fighting their battles,
Without a weapon, they know not they have.
Trying to gain knowledge,
Without the intelligence, they know not they have.
Looking for that spark, which already exists within them.

I weep for the world, building a mountain higher and higher.

Stage 5: Reflections; In And Out Of Duality

Turning away and running to another for help,
Does it help?
When messages come to them, to tell them something about themselves,
Do they know how to listen?
Looking for that clarity, which already exists within them.

I weep for the world, making it harder and harder.

Running helter-skelter looking for a cure,
When pain comes to the body, for a reason, because of a reason.
Taking them further away from true healing,
Looking for that cure outside of themselves,
Looking for that elixir, which already exists within them.

I weep for the world building a barrier, bigger and bigger.

Sorrows come to them, to teach them joy,
Hatred comes to them, to teach them love,

Misery comes to them, to teach them blessing,
Do they see? Do they realise?
Looking for that happiness, which already exists within them.

Wake up world! It is time to wake up!

It is time for mankind to attain supreme blessedness,
It is time to move towards the "Golden Era",
It is time we fully manifest into the gods that we truly are.

Wake up world! It is time to wake up.

Stage 5: Reflections; In And Out Of Duality

Upside-Down World

We live in an "Upside-Down" world.

Foods in their natural states as they are meant to be, are branded as "Organic" and priced higher.

Meditation is called "New Age", when it really is ancient and has been existing for thousands of years.

The natural healing systems which have been available since mankind existed, are categorised as "Complementary Therapies".

Infusing the body with "Synthetic Chemicals" is considered a fundamental form of treatment.

Living an unconscious zombie life is called "Normal".

Embracing yourself and showing to the world, who you really are, is called "Weird".

Mediocrity is the main form of acquiring knowledge from the "Outdated Systems", where true life skills are not taught.

Food is eaten as an indulgence and slowly damage oneself through over-indulgence and take "Plastic Remedy" to fix it.

Emotions are treated as "Default Programs" of the body, when truly they are in-built tools, internal guidance system.

You allow your mind to control you and then, go to see a "Shrink" to fix it from the outside, who themselves don't quite know how to harness the mind.

We live in an "Upside-Down" world.

Stage 5: Reflections; In And Out Of Duality

Wasted Day

A day without contemplation is a wasted day
A day without meditation is a wasted day
A day without appreciation is a wasted day
A day without connection is a wasted day
A day without intention is a wasted day
A day without sensation is a wasted day
A day without devotion is a wasted day

A day without gratitude is a wasted day
A day without passion is a wasted day
A day without forgiveness is a wasted day
A day without kindness is a wasted day
A day without compassion is a wasted day
A day without focus is a wasted day
A day without purpose is a wasted day

A day without giving is a wasted day
A day without receiving is a wasted day
A day without loving is a wasted day
A day without learning is a wasted day

A day without knowing is a wasted day
A day without healing is a wasted day
A day without growing is a wasted day

Stage 5: Reflections; In And Out Of Duality

What A Fool I Was!

I had a chalice to drink from,
It was filled with dirt.
I poured pure water, for, I was thirsty,
It turned muddy.
What a fool I was!

I was once a vessel,
Filled with impure thoughts,
I wanted to be pure and divine,
I received divine light, but it turned dark,
What a fool I was!

I had to be a fool,
To learn the valuable lessons of failure.
I had to be a fool,
To learn to clean the darkness that I was, to receive divine light,
I had to be a fool, to be awakened.

There Is Nothing Such As Wrong

There is nothing such as wrong.
When you say, "I know", the Universe agrees with you, "yes, you know".
When you say, "I don't know", the Universe agrees with you, "yes, you don't know".

Make a decision.
And go with it.
The universe unfolds all avenues for you to be your highest good.

There is nothing such as wrong.
Everything is right.
For, even when you make a mistake,
That's how you learn.

Stage 5

Reflections; In And Out Of Duality

As the fool continued on her journey, she revisited her physical memories, *'Memoirs Of Maggie'*.

The body that was in pain, that could not sleep at night and slept in the morning, so, 5 AM seemed like midnight. She was grumpy most mornings because of the heaviness. She remembered one such morning when her dog, who was her baby girl, Maggie, woke her up by barking aloud. She learnt a beautiful lesson that morning.

'No matter how annoying an experience in life,
Be open to see what it is waking you up to,
What unexpected beauty, it is showing you.
So, do not focus on the annoyance of life,

But look around and be open to see what it is trying to show you,
Something beautiful you don't want to miss.
The annoyance is just an alarm, so that you don't miss it.'

Many humans get upset when things do not go their way. When things do not go your way, instead of getting angry or disappointed, ask yourself, *'what is it showing me?'* Be open to see. Be willing. **There are lessons everywhere.** Whatever has come up is trying to show you something, that you would have missed, if it did not trigger you, you wouldn't have looked…and it may well be something beautiful that you never knew existed.

The fool was awakening. But she was still in a transitional stage. Transition meant, swinging between the old and the new ways. It was also the time for reflections, seeing the past with more clarity.

'Wrongs I Did'…she realised that all the wrongs she did, were wrongs done to herself. All the mistakes she made were created by her own fear and ignorance. All the anger

she had towards another, were anger towards herself. When she was harbouring all those fears, those resentments, those grudges, those feelings of lack and rejection, she was damaging herself, she was only doing wrong to herself. For many years of her life, she did what many people do, blame someone or something else for her misery. Then, she began to see that all those wrongs came from a place of neediness, a place of insecurity.

Often, humans blame others for wrongs that happen in their lives. It is always easier to blame someone else…your parents, your friends, your partner, your job, your government, your life. **But it is when you stop blaming others and start taking responsibility for yourself that you begin to see, that it is you who created that wrong.** That's when you begin to take your power back and begin to undo the wrongs in your life. That's when you start to walk from fear to strength, from needing love to love within, from ignorance to knowledge. That's when you start to see with clarity. That's when you start to heal. *'I did this'* **is a powerful realisation for transformation.**

'Mountain Of Lie'…the fool had learnt that by not living her truth, she was only lying to herself. Doing things, she did not want to do, being with people and in places she did not want to be.

'A mountain of lie,
It takes a long time to chisel.'

It was only because she was ignorant, because she was a fool. She forgave herself, for, that was the only way she could learn, through her mistakes. She had to be a fool first.

Now that she was beginning to see with clarity, she wanted to teach the world, share with others what she had learnt…how many wrongs she had done to herself, how many lies she had told herself…

'How to stay where you don't want to be, learn from me!
How to stay doing what you don't want to do, learn from me!'

…but it was important to make those mistakes, to speak those lies to herself, for her to be able to see the difference. To be able to see the good. **It is the realisation that is important.** Without that, you continue to build a mountain of lie, and live on that mountain, for many years, for many lifetimes.

'You Once Said' is about reflecting on the past…things that were said and comparing them to what she had begun to know. Distinguishing between the two kinds of *'love'*…love that she knew in the past, that was conditional, love that sprung from neediness and love that she had begun to know at that moment, love, that was pure energy. That is why two tenses are used in the same stanza.

> *You once said, you loved me.*
> *Did you know what love is?'*

Many people do not realise the true essence of the words they use and in that, they lie to themselves.

Pure love is always in the present. Situations may change, people may move on, but the energy of love is always present. **Because love is not about another, it is within you, it is everywhere, it is always here and now.** So is appreciation, so is respect, so is gratitude.

During the transitional phase, the fool was moving in and out between; the old way, which was dual in nature and the new way, which was becoming one with herself. During this time, there were so many thoughts, it was like being in a constant whirlwind, couldn't seem to stop…it was exhausting for her.

'Whirlwind Of Thoughts,
I can't seem to stop.'

It is a challenge for many who are on the path of awakening to keep the belief, the trust, that everything is working out. When you don't quite see the physical evidence yet, humans find it challenging to keep doing the work. **But it is important to keep the trust that you are a work in progress and that everything is in process, even when you do not see it.** No matter how fearful you get, how weary you feel, how angry you get, how anxious you feel, keep going. **It takes time to unveil what is hidden underneath so many layers of lies.** It takes time to chisel, but keep doing it, until you start to see the light from within.

Stage 5: Reflections; In And Out Of Duality

'Ho Ima! All I Wanted Was Love'…this was the time when the fool was looking back to her childhood, seeing what she couldn't see then. Remembering her own pain, losing her father at a tender age, wanting more time with her mother, but she was busy working to earn a living for the family. As a child, she could only feel her own pain of longingness, that, which she translated as love in her head. She could not see the pain her mother was going through. Her mother was fighting her own battle, trying to stay alive and feed her family, after losing her husband to physical mortality at a young age.

'Ho Ima! I wish you could see my heart,

For, you were engrossed in fighting your own pain.'

The fool was also remembering her brother's pain, who used to cut himself up often and finally ended up taking his own life…

'Ho Ima! I wish you could look at my cuts,

For, you were stabbed in your own heart.'

…at the same time, seeing her mother's pain in her heart, her own and her son's.

Wishing that there was more time as her mother's physical existence came to an end…

'Ho Ima! I wish we had more time,
For, you were kept in your own darkness.'

…seeing with clarity now, that her mother was in her own darkness, as her brother was, as she was. All wishing that life was easier.

'Ho Ima! I wish it was easier for us,
For, I know you wished life was a piece of cake.'

Then, realising that all they ever wanted was love.

'Ho Ima! All I wanted was love,
Ho Ima! All you wanted was love.'

Hence, the usage of the words *'I'* and *'you'*, meaning *'we'* as a collective.

Everyone goes through their own challenges, whether you know it or not, thus, the unified *'we'* to highlight that truth. **In those struggles, in the name of sorrow, insecurity, fear, all they seek is love.** But you remain in pain when you seek that love from the outside.

Many people fail to recognise the pain the other is going through, when they are suffering. Because they are busy seeking and expecting attention or sympathy. In that, they remain in their pain. When you stay expecting something from another, you cannot see beyond that, hence, you remain focussed on your pain.

As the fool became one with her spirit, knowledge began to flow through her. She started to see with such clarity, the veil that enveloped the world, the darkness that people lived in.

Lovers believe that they belong to one another. Parents get attached to their children, trying to own them, imposing their ideas on them, not allowing them to freely unfold into who they really are. Some parents hold them responsible for their happiness, blaming the child for their misery if the child does not turn out as they think they should. Some children blame their parents for the way they have turned out.

Each one of you play an important role in building a better tomorrow and that comes with awareness. That you as a human, are not here to procreate by default. When you decide to bring another human into the world, you sign a contract to reinvent yourself. What it means to become a parent is something many are not aware of. A parent does not own a child.

Your child is not a child, she is a soul.
You, as a mother, simply house her for nine months.
You, as a mother, are simply there to help her until she is ready.
But you get attached by giving it a label.
Let go when she is able.
This is by design, as nature intended it to be.'

You lead by example, not by control. You be, who you want your child to be. If you are not willing to do the inner work yourself, if you are not willing to change, how can you expect a change from another? That is *Your Contract When You Decide To Become A Parent'*. You, as a parent, are simply there to help, give support until the child is able.

This poem is also a message about teaching your children to be strong, to be independent, to be responsible, to be creative, to be joyful, to be compassionate because these are the characteristics of a soul, your true identity. Teaching is not just about sending them to a place of learning or pointing fingers at them or telling them to do

Stage 5: Reflections; In And Out Of Duality

this or that, but it is about living an example. You have to be that first, because without being, you do not know what it means to be that. Without being, you cannot show the way to another. **Only when you know from within can you teach another.**

'I Weep For The World'...the fool cried because she started to see that most people are going on living their lives without true knowledge, unwilling to go within, to find that knowledge. Not taking responsibilities for themselves, instead depending on others to fix their problems. Not learning the lessons, but procreating after procreating in darkness, building problem over problem.

'Wake up World! It is time to wake up!'

Many humans run to another human when they have pain in the body, looking for a cure outside of themselves. Pain comes to you for a reason, whether in the body or in your life. The cure lies within yourself. It is time to start learning to go within rather than depending on others and all things external. It is time to know that you come fully loaded with all the knowledge that you need, it is all in there within you, all the weapons to fight your battles, all the knowledge to evolve. It is time to truly manifest the powers you have within. **It is time to wake up.**

The fool cried that humans are asleep, living like zombies in a lifestyle they called *'normal'*. She cried for the *'Upside Down World'*.

The modern world of today, is controlled by more greed and less morals. Through greed they have polluted their own food with synthetic chemicals that are harmful for the natural human body. When these affect their bodies and give them illnesses, they run to another human who gives them even more *'man-made synthetic chemicals'* in the name of medication. Nature has all the medicines that you need. You have within you all the knowledge, all the medicines that you want. When each one of you learn to go within and do this work yourself, the world can be a different place. This is the only way to stop being controlled by those few who are driven by greed and hunger for power.

Stage 5: Reflections; In And Out Of Duality

Many humans numb themselves with unnatural things they consume by labelling them as *'food'*, *'drinks'*, *'medicine'* and *'happiness'*. They get programmed by things they watch, read, speak and hear, living an unconscious life. They go to acquire knowledge from a place, they call *'school'*, where they are taught to survive, not *'real life skills'*. It is an outdated system. They let their own minds to control them and then go to a *'shrink'* to fix it from the outside, who themselves do not quite know how to harness the power of the mind. It is an upside-down world.

In order to evolve, it is important to become aware that you are living in an upside-down world, that your system is outdated. For, without awareness, there is no hope for change. When you wake up to this realisation and start to seek the knowledge within, you are playing a part in creating a better future for humankind and for the planet.

'Wasted Day'…the fool saw how people wasted every single day, gone without an effort to learn and grow. Many believe that if they are busy doing a lot, their days are fruitful. However, if you are not spending time

working on yourself, going within, bringing your awareness to consciously practice kindness, compassion, gratitude, appreciation, love, learn, heal, grow, then, all those actions that keep you busy have no meaning.

'A day without growing is a wasted day'

Each day, people go on living without giving thanks for so many things that they are, and they receive. Each day, people go on living without forgiving, holding on to grudges, resentment, anger, bitterness, guilt and shame. Each day, people go on living without putting an effort to heal their lives, instead adding more to their pain.

All those days are wasted days because you are only adding more to your suffering, to your darkness and keeping yourself further away from the light.

As the fool learnt this, a profound moment of recognition unfolded for her, *'What A Fool I Was!'*

She was a clean vessel to begin with, but she dirtied herself with thoughts of sadness, rejection, hurt, bitterness, resentment and anger.

Stage 5: Reflections; In And Out Of Duality

You are all born pure and divine. But you muddy yourself with all the unnecessary information you gather through your outdated systems. You feed yourself with untrained thoughts which do you no good.

The fool then realised that she had to be a fool first to make those mistakes in order to learn the valuable lessons of failures, which led her to the knowing that…
'There is nothing such as wrong.
Everything is right.
For, even when you make a mistake,
That's how you learn.'
Hence, that, what you think is a mistake in life, a wrong in life, has a value. Therefore, nothing is wrong. **Everything is happening exactly as it is needed for your journey.**

The Universe responds to your vibration. Whatever you say, the Universe agrees with you, this is just the way it is. There is no discrimination, no judgement…no right or wrong, no good or bad…just is. Whatever you say, the Universe replies, *'Yes'*. Therefore, make a decision for yourself, about yourself, about your life and stick with it. Many people waver and that's why things do not unfold in the way they would like. You may say something to the Universe today, then something else tomorrow and another the day after. So, you see how easily things can go awry. But there is nothing such as wrong. Because you need to make those mistakes in order to learn.

It is only when you are not aware, do you remain in a loop of mistakes. You attract exactly as you are. **The more aware you become, the better you get in learning from your mistakes and grow.**

Stage 5: Reflections; In And Out Of Duality

Stage 6: Coming To The Light, Becoming A Spirit

Stage 6: Coming To The Light, Becoming A Spirit

Leaving The Matrix

I wrote poetry as a child.
I wrote poetry as a young woman.
I created art as a child.
I created art as a young woman.
I was one with me.

Then, I was tempted.
I entered the matrix,
Thinking it was real,
Thinking it was normal,
I stayed there for a long time.

But the clever soul started calling out to me,
"Hey there, come over here,
Here is real, rest is illusion".
Didn't know how to listen,
Kept living the matrix.
The call got louder,
The pain got stronger.
I was lost,

Stage 6: Coming To The Light, Becoming A Spirit

I was miserable,
I didn't know what to do.

I wished the pain would stop,
I wished the devil would quiet,
I wished I had someone who knew,
I wished I had guidance,
I wished I had clarity.

Then it happened, the lying serpent awakened,
The pain so great, was my guiding light,
The whispers in my ear taught me how to start listening,
The dreams in my sleep taught me how to start seeing,
The silence in my stillness taught me how to start unfolding.

I left the matrix.
I started writing poetry again.
I started creating art again.
I am now in harmony with me.
I now live the true reality.

[9] *Art Title: Shakti Serpent Awakening*

Stage 6: Coming To The Light, Becoming A Spirit

Everything Unfolds With Time

Every seed has in it, contained all the energy to grow.

The seed must remain in the dark for a time.
The embrace of the earth, the warmth of the soil,
The moist of rain, the purity of energy.

This darkness, although a challenge,
Is needed for the seed to break open,
For the seed to long for that light,
That longing so powerful, it builds the strength to emerge through the earth,
That yearning so mighty, it gives birth to the desire to shoot.

Every seed has in it, contained all the knowledge to expand.

The seed knows …
    …how many leaves to sprout,
    …how tall to rise,

…when to flower,
…when to fruit,
…when to die.

It is only a matter of time to unfurl,
For the seed, in all its glory.
Whether it's pain,
Whether it's joy,
Everything unfolds with time.

Every seed has in it, contained all the guidance to flourish.

Stage 6: Coming To The Light, Becoming A Spirit

[10] Art Title: Guidance Through Darkness

Everyone Is Going Through A Challenge

Everyone is going through a challenge.
No one's challenge is more or less.

While suffering, most think "my pain is worse than yours!"
While struggling, most think "my problem is bigger than theirs!"

Everyone is going through a challenge.
No one's pain is greater or smaller.

You get exactly what you need for your journey.
You are all at different stages.

Everyone is going through a challenge.
No one's journey is better or worse.

Some have physical pain,
Some have mental trouble and others emotional distress.

Stage 6: Coming To The Light, Becoming A Spirit

Everyone is going through a challenge.
No one's trouble is heavier or lighter.

You are quick to judge or blame another.
You forget they are fighting a battle just as you are.

Everyone is going through a challenge.
No one's battle is harder or easier.

Only One Purpose For Everyone

There is only one purpose for everyone,
to walk the journey from the outside to the inside,
to find who you really are.

For, when you find who you really are, you find the true essence of:
what it means to love and be love
what it means to be free from ignorance
what it means to heal your own pain
what it means to give birth to your own existence
what it means to serve yourself and others
what it means to become one with the Universe
what it means to grow and grow for eternity

Stage 6: Coming To The Light, Becoming A Spirit

---

[11] *Art Title: Your Centre Your True Essence*

I Have Come So Far

I have agreed, my Angels, to keep going.
I have come such a good way,
There's no turning back for me now.

I know the dark nights are getting over.
I can see the light, although faint,
I know that I can be the light itself one day.

I know the last steps are always the hardest ones.
So, please hold my hands as you have always done,
To take me to where the light is.

This path I am on, my Angels, I want to give it up at times.
For, it is a challenge so hard for a frail being like me,
But I know I won't give up as I have come so far.

Stage 6: Coming To The Light, Becoming A Spirit

Be The Spirit That You Are

I can no longer speak as a human, for, she no longer exists.
She has become one with the soul.
Therefore, she only speaks as a spirit.

I can no longer do the physical world, for, they mean nothing.
They mean nothing, for, you leave them all when you leave the body.
The only thing you take is the soul's learning.
The work you have started today, you carry forward.

I am no longer the human you think I am, for, she no longer exists.
She has become one with the soul.
Therefore, she only exists as a spirit.

I tried to be her but there was another path unfolding for her.

The more I tried to be her, the more conflict her body endured.
The best was to surrender, so here I am, at peace.

I tried to be a daughter and I tried to be a sister,
I tried to be a wife and I tried to be a friend,
The more I tried, the more the spirit cried.
For, I was weighing myself down with attachments,
I longed to be free, for, I am just a spirit, so here I am, free at last.

If you think, I have changed,
You knew just a little of me, before I became who I really am.
That you think I am, still exist, but that is only a part of me.
I can sing with you, I can dance with you, I can laugh with you.
I am this and…I am that…and also that…
For, I am a multi-dimensional being, for, I am a spirit.
I surrender to the spirit that I am.

Stage 6: Coming To The Light, Becoming A Spirit

And if you say that you are not a spirit, it is untrue.
It simply means that you have not found who you truly are.
You are more than one, just like I, and if you are just one,
It simply means that you do not know what you are.
Be the spirit that you are.

Stage 6
Coming To The Light, Becoming A Spirit

'Leaving The Matrix'

The fool had left the duality behind. She was now moving from the darkness of ignorance towards the light of knowledge. She was becoming one with herself, that once was.

'I wrote poetry as a child,
I wrote poetry as a young woman.
I created art as a child,
I created art as a young woman.
I was one with me.'

Stage 6: Coming To The Light, Becoming A Spirit

She was beginning to listen to the call of the soul. She had lived in an illusion, in a matrix for many years of her life. She didn't know how to listen to the true self. She was in pain. The pain got stronger and then it happened.

She learnt that the pain was much needed, it was her guiding light. There was no use for her to be in the matrix anymore, for, there was no need for her to go through the pain any longer. It had served its purpose of teaching her a beautiful lesson. That's why it came into her life. The moment the lesson was learnt, the pain was no longer required and was released. She left the matrix to fully unfold into who she really was, she was awakened.

I had now left the fool behind.

Many humans live in an illusion. They think it's real…the job, the family, the house…having all of those, living a normal life as they would say, living in the matrix. Then, pain comes to their lives and they don't know what went wrong. They wish it would go away. The mind gets louder. They do not know who to speak to. They do not know what to do.

'I wished the pain would stop,
I wished the devil would quiet,
I wished I had someone who knew,
I wished I had guidance,
I wished I had clarity.'

There is guidance everywhere…in your dreams, in your stillness…pain is your guiding light. When you know that pain comes for a reason, you learn to watch it, rather than suppress it, ignore it or avoid it. **When you learn to watch it, that's when you start to wake up. When you start to wake up, you begin to live your true reality.**

As I embarked on living the true reality, I began to appreciate the need for darkness, the duration of pain, of being a fool, to embrace that period, knowing that everything unfolded with time.

'It is only a matter of time to unfurl,
For the seed, in all its glory.
Whether it's pain,
Whether it's joy,'

'Everything Unfolds With Time' in the same way a seed does. A seed must remain in the darkness of the soil for it

to long for light. A seed must incubate in the warmth of the soil for a period, for it to break open. The darkness in the life of a human is the incubation period. **The longing to come out of the darkness is required to build the strength to emerge.** The desire so strong gives birth to the power to shoot out from the dark, into the light.

Each one of you is a seed. Within you, is contained all the knowledge for you to expand. Just as a seed knows exactly how many leaves to sprout, how tall to grow, when to flower, when to fruit and when to die; you know exactly when to do what. As the plant goes through different phases for each action, through different times, you have to go through your stages. It is only a matter of time for it all to unfold. What you have been nurturing defines what unfolds, whether it is joy or pain. **You have within you, all the guidance to flourish. You must allow the seed within you to grow into the abundant being that you are.**

When one is suffering, one tends to think that *'my pain in worse than yours!'* I used to do that too. When I was a fool, I thought I was the only one suffering compared to others. As I woke up, the perspective shifted. I started to see that *'everyone is going through a challenge'*. The reason why we get different doses of pain, different circumstances, is dependent on where we have been, what we have been doing to ourselves. This became my knowing…**you get exactly what you need in order to unlock your treasures.**

'Everyone One Is Going Through A Challenge.
No one's challenge is more or less.'

No matter what you are going through, no one's pain is greater or smaller. No pain is better or worse. Everyone goes through exactly what they need to go through in order to learn, in order to grow. When you know this from the core of your being, you can begin to learn to be kind to yourself and towards other's pain.

You get exactly what you need for your journey. Some may have physical pain, some mental, others may go through more emotional ordeals in their lives. You do not know what is going on with them. People are quick to judge. People are brisk to blame. You do not know what battles they are fighting, just as they do not know what you are enduring.

'Everyone is going through a challenge.
No one's battle is harder or easier.'

Stage 6: Coming To The Light, Becoming A Spirit

So, be kind to others and also, be kind to yourself. I was kind to others, but I was always beating myself up, with self-detrimental thoughts. When you innerstand this, you can learn to face a challenge with a smile and help others with joy.

When I was a fool, I constantly questioned myself, *'what is the purpose of my life?'* Like many, I thought we all have different purposes to fulfil. So, I kept questioning and every time I would stumble upon a challenge, I would tell myself that was the purpose for me. To fix whatever was the problem, was my purpose. This went on, for many years. It didn't fulfil me. In fact, most times it left me frustrated, trying to fix everything around me...people, life situations, etc. Finally, I had to give up trying to fix things outside of me. That frustration and unfulfillment pushed me to my journey inward simply because I had nowhere else to go. That's where I began to find the answers. That's when I started to see, that *'there is only one purpose for everyone, to walk the journey from the outside to the inside'*. That's where I found the real me. That's where I found true knowledge.

There is only one purpose for everyone, that is to find who you really are. In order to get there, one must do the inner work, to walk the journey from the outside to the inside. Because it is only when you find who you truly are, you begin to feel the true essence of everything…of love, of freedom, of healing, of your existence, of serving yourself and others, of becoming one with the Universe, of eternity.

When you transition from dark to light, there is a phase where the two meet, which contains both light and dark. This was the time when I was going through this phase, I was coming to the light, but not fully there yet, hence, the patches of darkness… *'I Have Come So Far'*.

'I have agreed, my Angels, to keep going.
I have come such a good way,
There's no turning back for me now.'

Those dark nights took me down, almost wanting to give up this journey I was on, but it was too late to give up. I had come a good way. I had come so far. I could only keep going forward. I made an agreement with myself. Every time it got a little harder, I reached out to my

Stage 6: Coming To The Light, Becoming A Spirit

Angels, asking them to hold my hands and take me to the light.

The reference, *'a good way'* is used rather than *'a long way'* because *'a long way'* implies a tiring, timebound journey. *'A good way'* refers to a timeless journey where things only get better and better as you keep going into the journey, towards the light, no matter how challenging it may seem or how long it may take.

'This path I am on, my Angels, I want to give it up at times.
For, it is a challenge so hard for a frail being like me,
But I know I won't give up as I have come so far.'

When you are on your path of awakening, no matter how arduous it may seem, never give up. No matter how many times you fall, keep getting up. Ask for help, your Angels, your guides are always there to help you. **As long as you keep going, no matter how challenging it seems, you can get there one day.**

As I went deeper into my journey within, I started to see my outside crumbling.

That, which I thought was my reality…to be a daughter, a sister, a wife, a human was all an illusion. They no longer meant anything to me. I became one with the soul. Therefore, I began to speak as a spirit… *'Be The Spirit That You Are'*.

'I can no longer speak as a human, for, she no longer exists.
She has become one with the soul.
Therefore, she only speaks as a spirit.'

People collect physical things, but they mean nothing as you leave them all when you leave the body. We even leave the physical body that we identify ourselves with while we are alive. **The only thing that you take as a spirit is the soul's learning and that is what you carry forward. What you have started today can never be lost.**

Stage 6: Coming To The Light, Becoming A Spirit

I tried to be just a human, but the more I tried, the more my body cried out because of the conflict between the outside and the inside. The soul was calling out to me. Finally, I learnt to surrender and only after that, did I find peace. Only then did I find my true freedom, free from all attachments.

'I tried to be a daughter and I tried to be a sister,
I tried to be a wife and I tried to be a friend,
The more I tried, the more the spirit cried.
For, I was weighing myself down with attachments,
I longed to be free, for, I am just a spirit, so here I am, free at last.'

Humans give much importance to labels…they are either, a mother, a father, a sister, a brother, a son, a daughter, a family, a friend, a society, a country, a religion, a colour, a race. You are just weighing yourself down with all these labels which are attached to some duties. Because each one comes with an obligation to fulfil, an image you have to live up to. You are not free; you cannot be free when you have so many expectations to live up to. You live in the bondage of attachment, what you call *'love'* is living in the bondage of duties. **It is only when you learn to truly free yourself, can your society, your country, your planet become free from suffering.**

It starts with you. Be the free spirit that you are to free humankind.

As I evolved from who I was to who I was becoming, people who knew me in the past said I had changed. They only knew a part of me, I was unfolding fully into who I really am, the multi-dimensional spirit. I am not the only one who is multi-dimensional, you are too. Everyone is.

'And if you say that you are not a spirit, it is untrue.
It simply means that you have not found who you truly are.
You are more than one, just like I, and if you are just one,
It simply means that you do not know what you are.
Be the spirit that you are.'

Stage 6: Coming To The Light, Becoming A Spirit

Stage 7: The Beginning Of Divine Guidance

Stage 7: The Beginning Of Divine Guidance

Phee-Bi's Magic

My name is Phee-Bi and this is my story.

I wasn't born with wings.
I was born "normal" just like you.
I went through a lot of suffering for years.

---

[12] *Art Title: Phee-Bi's Magic*

Stage 7: The Beginning Of Divine Guidance

Fed up with so much physical pain,
Fed up with so much mental agony,
I broke down and cried one night...
"Dear God, why do I suffer so much?
If you really exist, help me?
Show yourself to me?"

There appeared a big bright light.
A huge golden white light,
I didn't know what it was,
But I had no fear.
I asked, "what are you?"

A voice boomed through the light...
"It is I, that you call "God" or "Angels" or " Source Energy".

"What do you mean by Source Energy?"

"I am the source of all the energy that you are.
I am the source of all the light that you are.
It is from this energy you are made.

We are one."

"What does that mean?"

"It means that you are energy.
It means that you are not fixed.
It means that you can change whatever you want,
whenever you wish.
You can create your own reality.
It means that you are a light being,
Who has enough light to shine upon any darkness."

"So, how do I find my light?"

"Simple! Just pull out the unwanted weeds in the garden of your mind.
The beauty is there in all its splendour.
Allow only the seeds you want growing in your garden.
And nurture them, love them.
Before you know it, you can be shining your light".

...and the bright light vanished.

Stage 7: The Beginning Of Divine Guidance

"It took me some time to clear the weeds,
But the message was right.
I wanted beautiful translucent butterfly wings.
I started growing one.
I created them.
I am pure energy.
I am pure light.

Gratitude fills my heart.
I found my magic!"

My Angels

You fluttered your wings into my ear,
When I could hear no one.

You wrapped your arms around me,
When I cried in solitude.

You lighted my path,
When I was lost.

You showered me with unconditional love,
When I received love from no one.

You blessed me with divine healing,
When I was dense with pain.

You taught me forgiveness,
When I was hurt.

You filled my heart with gratitude,
When I didn't appreciate.

Stage 7: The Beginning Of Divine Guidance

You dispensed unparallel wisdom,
When I was a fool.

You bestowed upon me transcendental guidance,
When I was seeking.

You led me to a magical way,
When I couldn't trust.

My Angels, you held my hands,
To bring me to where I am,
To a place of boundless joy,
To a place of ethereal beauty,
To a place of blissful calm.

Shine Your Light

You are a light being.
You have it in there.
Shine your light.

It is so much easier to be in a place you don't want to be and never take a risk.
It is so much easier to accept defeat and never try.
It is so much easier to be in pain and never revive.

It is a challenge to live your dream.
It is a challenge to listen to your heart.
It is a challenge to heal.

Yes, it takes a lot of practice.
Yes, it takes a lot of strength.
Yes, it takes a lot of love.

It is so much easier to be in the dark and never shine.
It is so much easier to stay the same and never grow.

Stage 7: The Beginning Of Divine Guidance

It is so much easier to remain scared and never feel true joy.

Yes, it requires a lot of desire.
Yes, it requires a lot of contemplation.
Yes, it requires a lot of intentness.

It is so much easier to stay in your comfort and never know who you truly are.
It is so much easier to stay in fear and never take the step to become who you truly are.
It is so much easier to stay in suffering and never feel the blessing.

Yes, change is uncomfortable.
Yes, change is demanding.
Yes, change is painful.

But you are a light being.
You have it in there.
Shine your light.

The Rise Of The Goddess Consciousness

Rise to the power that you are

Not driven by greed

Not driven by ego

Not driven by hunger

But from the purity of love that you are

Be the Goddess that you are

You are the power that you don't know exists within you

You are a mighty creator in this magnificent cosmos

---

[13] *Art Title: Rise Of The Goddess Consciousness*

Stage 7: The Beginning Of Divine Guidance

You are supreme love
You are touching light

Oh women! you are mighty inspiration
Oh women! you are the centre of the Universe
Oh women! come embody your true light
It is time to rise to the Goddess Consciousness

Stage 7
The Beginning Of Divine Guidance

'Phee-Bi's Magic'

In one of those dark nights, in pain, in frustration, I cried out,

"Dear God, why do I suffer so much?
If you really exist, help me?
Show yourself to me?"

A big golden white light appeared in my room. It was oval in shape, from the floor to the ceiling. I say 'golden white light' because the outer rays were golden like the Sun, but the inner was white. It was bright, should've been blinding, but it wasn't. A voice spoke to me.

Source Energy came to my call to give me guidance. Said to me, 'you are all energy beings made from the same

Stage 7: The Beginning Of Divine Guidance

source, we are one. It means that you are changeable at all times, you do not have to remain fixed, you can create your own reality. It means that you are made of light, a fragment of this light and within you is the same power that created the Universe. Each one of you has enough light to shine upon any darkness. You do not have to do anything to get to the light because it is always there. **All you have to do is pull out the weeds from your mind.** Unknowingly, you feed yourselves with a lot of heaviness that darkens your own light. Once you become aware, you start to release the darkness and you automatically start to shine'.

It took me some time to make sense of this and apply it in my life. The guidance was right. I started to create my own magic.

'It took me some time to clear the weeds,

But the message was right.

I wanted beautiful translucent butterfly wings.

I started growing one.

I created them.

I am pure energy.

I am pure light.'

From then on, I started hearing more messages from my guides... *'My Angels'*.

'You fluttered your wings into my ear,
When I could hear no one.'

My Angels...they sang to me; they called me by my name. They brought me back into my body when I left it in suffering. You may not know your Guardian Angels and Spirit Guides, but they know you by your name. They are always there for you. Trust.

My Angels...they taught me how to be pure love, they taught me about healing, about forgiveness, about gratitude. They bestowed on me all the wisdom I didn't know I was seeking and they taught me how to trust the Universe completely.

I started seeing more of my own light. I learnt to transmute my own darkness to become the light. My Angels, they held my hands and brought me to this place where there is pure love, boundless joy, real beauty and bliss every day, every moment. I trusted, I didn't give up and they led me to a magical place.

'My Angels, you held my hands,
To bring me to where I am,

Stage 7: The Beginning Of Divine Guidance

To a place of boundless joy,
To a place of ethereal beauty,
To a place of blissful calm.'

Most humans love conditionally because they have not learnt how to be love. Most find it impossible to forgive when they feel someone has wronged them. Many find it unable to appreciate and be grateful for experiences that are unpleasant. **But it is when you innerstand and practice the true meaning of love, gratitude and forgiveness that you really learn to clean yourself out.** That's when you learn to heal yourself, that's when you can get into a state of unlimited joy and blissful calm.

Yes, it was a challenge to pursue my dreams. Yes, it was a challenge to listen to my heart. Yes, it was a challenge to learn to heal my body. Yes, it was uncomfortable to change.

I didn't know what it meant by *'Shine Your Light'*. When I was a fool, I stayed in fear, I stayed in darkness, I stayed in suffering for so many years. That was my comfort zone.

Many people stay in their comfort zones for a long, long, time…some realise, many do not, many stay there for their entire lives, many lifetimes. **Comfort keeps you in the same state.** You cannot heal, you cannot grow. It is so much easier to stay the same and never grow. Because it takes a lot of practice, a lot of desire and a lot of strength to step out of your comfort zone to take a risk. Adventure is not comfortable. But when you remain comfortable, you cannot learn to shine, you cannot experience true joy.

'It is so much easier to stay in your comfort and never know who you truly are.

It is so much easier to stay in fear and never take the step to become who you truly are.

It is so much easier to stay in suffering and never feel the blessing.'

You are a light being, you have it in there. You can do it. You can shine your light. **It is now time to rise to that light.** It is now time to spread the message. It is time to rise to the Goddess Consciousness.

'The Rise Of The Goddess Consciousness'…is a message to focus on the need to wake up to the feminine energy that

Stage 7: The Beginning Of Divine Guidance

exists within each one of you, not just women, but men too. Masculine and feminine energies exist within all. The world has been gripped in an imbalanced masculine energy for centuries…represented by the wars, the rise and control of the world by capitalism, ruthlessness, division, the greed for power and money.

Through this guidance, the Universe is letting you know that it is time for humankind to move into the softer, more creative, more intuitive, more nurturing, healing feminine energy which is an embodiment of oneness. **It is time to move into this space of inspiration and become the creators that you are, the love and light that you are, the unity consciousness that you are.**

'Be the Goddess that you are
You are the power that you don't know exists within you
You are a mighty creator in this magnificent cosmos
You are supreme love
You are touching light'

However, it is important to remember that the feminine energy can also become imbalanced if driven by greed or hunger. **It must come from the purity of love that you are.**

This is also a special message for women. Many are not aware that they are the centre of their Universe, which means that they hold a responsible position. **When women on this planet begin to activate this wisdom and embody their true light, that is when an exponential shift can happen in human evolution.** It is time for the true power of love to shine, it is time to rise to the Goddess Consciousness.

The creative energy is feminine…conceptualisation, conception and creation are feminine energies. Realisation, execution and action are masculine energies. They are complementary. They are yin and yang. One is no more or no less. They both have roles to play. Both are incomplete without the other. However, for the execution to happen in a beneficial way for the pure good of all, the conceptualisation must first be in that order, only then can it unfold into the beautiful creation that it is meant to be. Everyone must see this from the core of their being.

Stage 7: The Beginning Of Divine Guidance

Stage 8: Receiving With Absolute Clarity

Stage 8: Receiving With Absolute Clarity

You Must Have It And Lose It

I had it when I was born,
But I didn't know I had it.
I had to lose it, to know I had it,
So, I could find it again.

I knew myself when I was born,
But I didn't know I knew myself.
I had to lose myself, to know I knew myself,
So, I could discover myself again.

I was love when I was born,
But I didn't know I was love.
I had to lose love, to know I was love,
So, I could seek love again.

I was courage when I was born,
But I didn't know I was courage.
I had to lose courage, to know I was courage,
So, I could treasure courage again.

Stage 8: Receiving With Absolute Clarity

I was innocent when I was born,
But I didn't know I was innocent.
I had to lose innocence, to know I was innocent,
So, I could become innocent again.

You must have it and lose it,
To want to find it again,
For, you cry tears of joy, when you find it again.

14

Love Is An Energy

Love is an energy…
    …that transcends through time
    …that lights through darkness
    …that propels through barriers

Love is an energy…
    …that dissolves all bitterness
    …that heals all pain
    …that transmutes all fear

---

14 Art Title: Anahata Energy

Stage 8: Receiving With Absolute Clarity

Love is an energy…

    …that revitalises the body

    …that comforts the mind

    …that satiates the soul

Love is an energy…

    …that boosts your power

    …that fuels your passion

    …that creates your reality

Love is an energy…

    …that releases your past

    …that grounds your present

    …that writes your future

Love Without

Love without expectations
Love without boundaries
Love without labels

Love without envy
Love without struggle
Love without grudges

Love without imposing
Love without possessing
Love without obsessing

Love without depending
Love without needing
Love without uncertainty

Love without guilt
Love without denials
Love without conditions

Stage 8: Receiving With Absolute Clarity

Love without limitations
Love without physicality
Love without attachments

Love because you are love
Love because that's the only way to be
Love because that's who you are through eternity

One Heart Has All The Love To Heal The Entire Planet

One heart has all the love to heal the entire planet
One teardrop is all it takes to wash all pain
One laughter is all it takes to fill the entire world with joy
One thought is all it takes to allow wonderful creation
One emotion is all it takes to fire your undeniable passion
One song is all it takes to move the longing soul
One dance is all it takes to raise you up higher
One kindness is all it takes to reassure humanity
One generosity is all it takes to uplift one another
One realisation is all it takes to go through the journey
One courage is all it takes to build the planet
One strength is all it takes to douse weaknesses
One desire is all it takes to grow
One light is all it takes to illuminate all darkness
One knowledge is all it takes to extinguish all ignorance
One love is all it takes to remove all fear
One heart has all the love to heal the entire planet

Stage 8: Receiving With Absolute Clarity

15

---

[15] *Art Title: One Heart Network*

Compassion

Compassion is not just about loving others,
Compassion is not just about understanding others,
Compassion is not just about helping others,

Compassion is about innerstanding them, even when you know what they've done is not right, even when you don't benefit from doing so.

Compassion is about being tender, even when you are met with harshness, knowing that anger is a fire that slowly burns you.

Compassion is about maintaining calm, even when you don't get what you expected and still hold a fair mind towards them.

Compassion is about forgiving them even when you are hurt, knowing that all pain come from ignorance.

Stage 8: Receiving With Absolute Clarity

Compassion is about being kind, even when you are perplexed, it is about being able to put yourself in their shoes.

Compassion is about being generous, even when you receive nothing in return, knowing that this is a bountiful world.

Compassion is about nurturing, even when you know it is a challenge sometimes, even when you may not enjoy the fruit of your labour.

Compassion is about holding a space for them, even when you know they are gone, even when they are not with you, in body or in spirit.

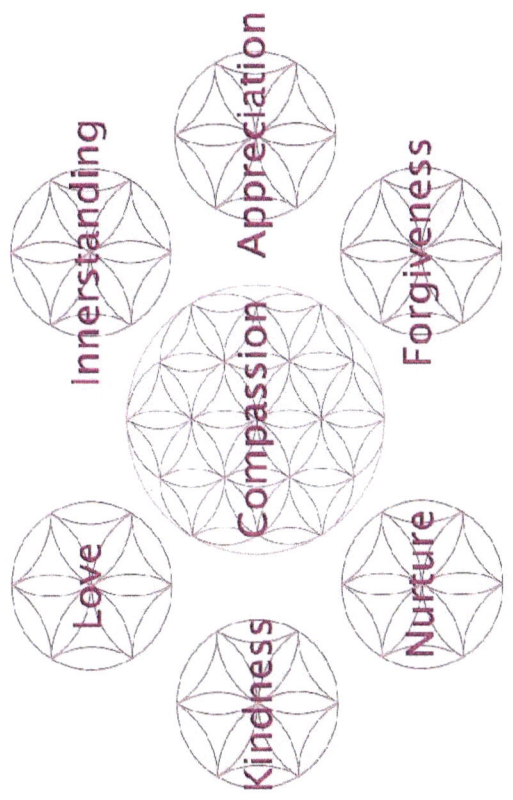

[16] *Art Title: Six Petals Of Compassion*

Stage 8: Receiving With Absolute Clarity

Butterfly Song

I am truly happy with myself.
I am truly happy with where I am.

Yes, I had to go through darkness.
Yes, I had to be stuck in one place.

But it is the misery of being stuck in darkness that gave me the desire to be light.
But it is the pain of being stuck in one place that gave me the desire to fly.

---

[17] *Art Title: Lightworker*

Words Through A Soul

I have come a good way.
I have learnt a good deal.

I wanted to be free.
I wanted wonderful wings.

I waited, for, I knew it would happen.
I waited, for, I trusted the process.

And now I emerge a beautiful butterfly.
And now I evolve to who I really am.

I am truly happy with myself.
I am truly happy with where I am.

Stage 8: Receiving With Absolute Clarity

I'm Proud Of Me

We struggle to truly love each other while we live.
We find ways and means to bicker with one another.
We forget we are mortals.
We die soon before we know it.
We wish we had more time.
We wish we loved more.

They say your entire life flashes just before you leave the body.
Would you rather see love and joy?
Would you rather see anger over trivial matters?
Would you rather see hatred that burnt your body?

No matter how important you think it is.
If it isn't spiritual, it is physical.
If it is physical, it is material.
There's nothing you take from the physical.
There's no material you carry to the next realm.

What you carry, are love and joy.

Words Through A Soul

What you carry, are anger and hatred.
Would you rather carry love?
Would you rather carry hatred?

So much energy is wasted on anger.
So much toxicity is created from hatred.
It burns the entire planet.

Nothing matters but love and forgiveness.
All else is futile.
Learn to let go and forgive.
Learn to love every moment.
For, life comes with an expiry date.

Live with so much compassion,
Live with forgiveness,
Live with gratitude,
That, when life flashes your story before you leave the body,
You smile and say, "I'm proud of me".

Stage 8: Receiving With Absolute Clarity

Feels Good To Be Home

When you find the true self,
You are home.

Even when you are lost,
It doesn't take long to find your way back.

Even when you go through pain,
It doesn't take time to heal.

That feeling of being home,
Because you know you're only truly happy with yourself.

You are happy to have your time by yourself,
Because you know you can create in that solitude.

You are pleased to have the time to reconnect with yourself,
Because you know you can hear the soul's voice.

Feels good to be home.
The feeling of safety lies within,
The feeling of stability,
It's all within, not without.

Stage 8: Receiving With Absolute Clarity

My Union And My Duality

I was weak, I was needy.
I wanted to be strong, I wanted to be independent.
I am strong, I am independent.
I jump in and out between my union and my duality; and that's fine.
I have been transitioning from being frail to a powerful being.

I was stuck, I was suffering.
I wanted to be free, I wanted to be joy.
I am free, I am joy.
I jump in and out between my union and my duality; and that's fine.
I have been transitioning from being a human to a spiritual being.

I was sad, I was depressed.
I wanted to be cheerful, I wanted to be hopeful.
I am cheerful, I am hopeful.

I jump in and out between my union and my duality; and that's fine.

I have been transitioning from being distant to a blissful union.

I was lost, I was full of doubt.
I wanted to be found, I wanted to be pure.
I am found, I am pure.
I jump in and out between my union and my duality; and that's fine.
I have been transitioning from being "just alive" to living a life of purpose.

I was lonely, I was overwhelmed.
I wanted to be love, I wanted to be calm.
I am love, I am calm.
I jump in and out between my union and my duality; and that's fine.
I have been transitioning from being naïve to mastery.

Stage 8: Receiving With Absolute Clarity

The Art Of Surrender

Source: Why don't you trust and come with me where I am guiding you?

Persona: I cannot, for, I have seen much pain, I have suffered far too much.

Source: Why do you focus on what's been? What you've seen is done and gone? Why can't you focus on what's coming? The beautiful future, which is like an unmoulded clay, fresh and ready to mould into whatever shape you'd like it to be.

Persona: Because I cannot see. I can only focus on what I can see.

Persona: Show me what I can do in my future and I'll believe you.

Source: But that's the beauty of the future, you cannot see it because it does not exist yet. You have the power to create whatever you want.

Wouldn't you like a blank canvas, so that you can paint on it, whatever you wish? If I gave you a canvas which is already filled with colours, tell me, would you be happy? And what if you don't like what I have painted for you, you would throw it away, wouldn't you? That's the power of free will. Creation has left it for you to create your own landscapes.

Persona: I am laden with heavy weights on my shoulder, I cannot do anything else. If only, someone would carry for me, I can be light and focus on creating my future?

Source: Why don't you let me carry your weights? All you have to do is, put them down and trust that I am going to carry them for you. All you have to do is, surrender to that knowing and you can travel light.

Persona: How do I know I can trust you? How do I know you will carry them for me?

Stage 8: Receiving With Absolute Clarity

Source: How do you breathe? Do you trust that air is always there for you?

How were you conceived in your mother's womb without your doing?

How does your body function?

Do you know that life force which flows through you, keeps you alive?

Do you know there is unseen guidance available for all?

How do all these things happen without your knowing? Isn't it trust?

Did you say, "I will not come through my mother because I do not trust the process"?

Did you say, "I do not trust there's air so I will not breathe", before taking your first breath?

Did you say, "I will not eat because I do not know how to", before swallowing your first morsel of food?

When you plant a seed, do you say, "I won't sow it because it looks different from the plant I want?"

You know exactly how that seed can grow, the plant it is to become.

You grow it with trust, you nurture it with love, that it is going to flower and fruit, as it is by design, at the right time.

Everything exists for you and in you. When you learn to recognise this and surrender to the process, that everything is working out by design, that's when you learn to travel light. That's when you heal. That's when you grow.

Stage 8: Receiving With Absolute Clarity

Life Is In Surrender

Life is in surrender
Not in control

Life is in allowing
Not in restraint

Life is in trust
Not in doubt

Life is in attraction
Not in repulsion

Life is in expansion
Not in contraction

The Power Of Growth

The power of growth, it breaks through barriers
The power of growth, nothing can stop you
The power of growth, nothing can keep you down

All you need, is the dream to grow
        …the desire to grow
        …the intention to grow
By design, you must expand
By design, you must flourish
By design, you must create
All you need, is to learn the art of allowing
        …to learn the art of surrender
        …to learn the art of receiving

The power of growth, it erases all agony
The power of growth, it releases all the past
The power of growth, it teaches all life lessons

Stage 8: Receiving With Absolute Clarity

Rumble's Jenna

In a beautiful village called Efil,
There lived two men.
One was called Rumble, the other Russ.

Both loved gardening more than anything else,
spending hours with their plants,
fussing over their flowers.

Both loved admiring the beautiful butterflies,
watching the busy bees,
chatting to the brilliant birds.

They gave thanks to the rain, to the earth, to the gods.

Then, life happened.
They were put to the test.
There was Rumble and there was Russ.

Both had a plant each that was diseased,
the same symptoms,

the same feelings.

Rumble loved his plant so dear; he didn't want her to die.

He spent hours, he spent days, looking after her,
putting all his attention to that one dying plant.
He was sad, he was going to lose her,
Angrily he asked the gods, "why is this happening"?

He didn't want to lose the plant; she was rare to find,
she was precious to him,
couldn't think of a life without her,
even gave her a name, called her, "Jenna".

He spent hours, he spent days, neglecting the rest,
didn't realise days were gone,
weeks were gone.

He moped and he moaned about the dying plant,
didn't realise months were gone.
didn't realise his garden was gone.

Stage 8: Receiving With Absolute Clarity

Rumble lost his garden.

He lost the will to live,
couldn't think of planting another garden,
dreaded the loss again.

He lost the joy in his life,
lost the spark of his existence.

He lost his life.

Russ loved his plant so dear; he didn't want her to die.

But he knew, he had to let go.

He learnt that nothing lasts forever,
that life comes and goes,
that it is for a reason.

He learnt that he can cherish the memories,
that everything falls away when they no longer serve.

He learnt to focus on what he's got,
to appreciate what he has,
to be grateful for everything, for the dying and the growing.

He learnt to trust the process,
to love the entirety of creation.

He nurtured all his plants, fed them, watered them, spoke to them, loved them.
His garden flourished and blossomed.

Russ thrived with his garden.

Joy continued to fill his life.

One fine summer's day, he went to the farmer's market.
He found a special someone selling the same plant that he lost to the disease some years ago.
She was as enchanting as the plant itself.
Yes, it was rare, but here it was again, as if sent by the gods themselves.

Stage 8: Receiving With Absolute Clarity

Yes, it was precious, and it was meant just for him.

He remembered how his old friend, Rumble, loved that plant so dear.

He gave a heartfelt gratitude to the special lady as he paid her for the plant.

He asked her name as he was saying goodbye, she replied, "Jenna".

He planted Jenna in his garden in the memory of his old friend, Rumble.

[18] *Art Title: Rumble's Jenna*

Stage 8: Receiving With Absolute Clarity

So Much, You Know Not

There is so much potential,
You know not.
There is so much creativity,
You know not.
There is so much depth,
You know not.
There is so much knowledge,
You know not.
There is so much help,
You know not.
There is so much guidance,
You know not.
There is so much abundance,
You know not.
There is so much grace,
You know not.
There is so much love,
You know not.

Stage 8

Receiving With Absolute Clarity

I started to receive with absolute clarity, the deeper meaning of all, the truth from the Universe. The veil of ignorance was lifted.

'You must have it and lose it,
To want to find it again,
For, you cry tears of joy, when you find it again.'

I was love, I was courage, I was innocent...I had it all, but I didn't know. So, I lost it. But now, I know that I had to lose it to want to find it again, for, when you find it knowingly, that's when you truly appreciate and nurture it.

Stage 8: Receiving With Absolute Clarity

'I had it when I was born,
But I didn't know I had it.'

You are born fully loaded with every information you need for your existence. But you must lose it, to truly know the value of it. A simple example...most humans value health after experiencing illnesses. **The absence of a quality highlights the value it had in your life.** Hence, the losing has a merit. It is to show you exactly what you had, what you were born with. So, do not fret when you lose a part of you, it is only to stir up the desire within you to want to find it again. For, you are filled with true joy when you find it again, and this time you know the value, so, you nurture it for life. This is the difference between ignorance and knowing. When you live in ignorance, you live under a veil, in darkness. **When you do everything from a place of knowing, nothing is random, all is crystal clear.**

When I was a fool, I thought love meant loving somebody, loving something, being attached to another. I kept saying, all I want is love, not riches, not recognition, nothing fancy, just a simple life of love. I thought, it can't be hard to achieve that. But oh yes! Was it hard! I was looking for love in all the wrong places. I was looking for love from another. So, I couldn't get it. I was only met with hurt after hurt. Finally, when I broke down, stopped looking on the outside and started going inward, I found that love I was looking for. It was within me all the time.

My inner guidance was telling me all along, *'the love you want exists'*. I heard that bit, but I didn't hear the second part...that is, *'it exists within you'*. So, I kept looking for it outside of me. I knew the *'what'*, but I didn't know the *'where'*. I had to go through the hurt to point me in the right direction. As I started on my journey inward, it started to unfold for me that I had all the knowledge within me, I had all the love within me. I just didn't know I had it.

Stage 8: Receiving With Absolute Clarity

'Love is an energy...
 ...that transcends through time
 ...that lights through darkness
 ...that propels through barriers'

Love is a power that diffuses all darkness and propels through barriers. Not the love, the fool thought it was, it has nothing to do with another. It is just an energy that is within you, with you, around you, all the time. **Love is an energy that heals all pain and transmutes all fear.** If worries, anxieties, fears are dominant in your life, it only means that you are not tuning into the love energy that exists within you. If you are trapped in pain from your past or trepidations about the future, it only means that you are not connecting to the love that you are. When you truly start to feel and connect to the energy of love, you realise that it is all you need to dissolve all bitterness and revitalise your body, rejuvenate your life. It is the energy that releases your past and heals you. **When you learn how to heal, you know exactly what is happening, you are grounded in your present and you have no worries about your future because you know that you have got it.**

It takes some time to practice it, it takes some time to learn to listen to the guidance, but have patience, keep doing the work. Little by little, it unfolds for you, *'the what's* and *'the where's'*.

'Love Without' expectations, without labels. Many people love from a place of neediness, or conditions, just as the fool did, but that isn't love. That is dependency. That is conditional. Many people also try to possess each other in the name of love. Some love because they feel guilty about something they have done. Many love because they are obsessed with another, and others love because they feel happy to be in control. None of these are love. Love without any limitations, without any attachments. All the people and things you get attached to; they all disappear one day. No matter how much you say you love them, you cannot take them with you when you transition from your physical body. You cannot take any of them into your next phase.

'Love because you are love
Love because that's the only way to be
Love because that's who you are through eternity'

Stage 8: Receiving With Absolute Clarity

Love because you are love. That is the true essence of love. Just be love. **When you are connected to the true energy of love that you are, that's the knowledge you carry forward through time, that's when you see everybody and everything with love, that's when you do everything from a place of love.** You become love.

When you tune into that love, it only takes one to set off a ripple effect. **One heart is a powerful transmitter of this beautiful sequence.** When you focus on being that love to truly heal yourself, you become the beacon, that is passed from one to another and to another, lighting the entire planet. **One heart has all the love to heal the entire planet.** That one tear has to start, to wash away all pain; that one laughter, truly from the heart, to fill the world with joy; that one kindness to reassure humanity; that one realisation to put you in the right direction; that one knowledge to extinguish all ignorance; that one love to remove all fear and that one light to illuminate all darkness. **When you start to be that one, the light spreads.**

'One light is all it takes to illuminate all darkness
One knowledge is all it takes to extinguish all ignorance

One love is all it takes to remove all fear
One heart has all the love to heal the entire planet'

When you are that love, you are an embodiment of true *'Compassion'*.

'Compassion is not just about loving others,
Compassion is not just about understanding others,
Compassion is not just about helping others,'

Compassion is not just about feeling for another or helping another. It is not just about understanding others, but it is about innerstanding them, even when you know what they have done is not right, even when you do not benefit from doing so. It is about being tender even when you are met with anger and harshness, knowing that anger is an energy that only burns oneself. Tenderness is all you need to share as a compassionate one to help soothe them. It is about being calm even when you do not get what you expected because you know why it happened the way it happened; therefore, you hold an unbiased neutral space. Thus, maintaining a non-reactionary mind. Because you know that when you expect, you are attaching an energy,

Stage 8: Receiving With Absolute Clarity

a desire, an emotional reaction to a person or a situation which only leads to disappointment, when not met.

Compassion is about forgiving those who may have hurt you, knowing that the reason why they hurt others is only because of their own wound which stems from ignorance. So, they couldn't have known any better. In that knowing, you forgive them.

Compassion is about being able to put yourself in their shoes in empathy, even when you don't know why it has happened. Because deep inside, you know that there is a reason behind everything. It is about being generous, even when you do not receive anything in return from the person you have given to. It is about giving without any expectation because you know that this is an abundant Universe you live in; you do not have to expect. What goes, comes back to you, it may not necessarily be from the same people, but it finds its way to you. It is about nurturing your journey, being compassionate even when you find it challenging, even when you do not see the fruits of your labour, even when you feel like giving up on those dark nights, you still choose to continue gently, kindly. It is about holding a space for others even when they are not physically or spiritually with you. Many people find it impossible to have good thoughts or hold good intentions for those who do not live up to their ideals. Many judge others based on their made-up mental or social scales. They may not be where you are or where you think they should be, but you can still learn to show compassion by holding them in good intentions, knowing that they are going through challenges that you may or may not be aware of. That is true compassion.

Compassion is not about your feelings for another. It is about being. Be compassion. Be love.

In that love, you are truly one with yourself. In that oneness, you are truly happy with yourself. In that happiness, you are truly free.

'Butterfly Song'
'I wanted to be free.
I wanted wonderful wings.'

One has to go through darkness to give birth to the desire to be the light. One has to go through the pain of being stuck to want to fly.

I started to see there was merit in pain. There were lessons to be learnt.

'I have come a good way.
I have learnt a good deal.'

Lessons that help you evolve, to transform into the magic that you are. **But you must have patience, you must learn to trust, which, in itself, is another lesson.** When you learn this, you become the magic. You become who you really are.

'And now I emerge a beautiful butterfly.
And now I evolve to who I really am.'

That's when you live with compassion, with forgiveness, with gratitude, with love, from the place of *'being'*. **That's when you become *'The Energy Being'* that you are.** That's when you say, *'I'm Proud Of Me'*.

Many people spend their time in their human bodies as if they are immortals. They bicker over petty reasons, they collect material things, they fill up their bodies with anger and hatred, not knowing that they are damaging themselves and the planet. They spend their entire lives doing all the things they do not want to do, being the person, they do not want to be and then, when the day comes, when they have to leave the physical body, the last moment is filled with regret. You cannot carry the physical things, not the people you hold dear, not even your own body; you only carry your memories locked into the soul.

'Would you rather carry love?
Would you rather carry hatred?'

Every vibration you emit as an energy being, contributes to the collective energy of the planet. Anger is an intense energy and can be put to good use, but it is wasted when you take it out on another. So much hatred for another person, race, classification, country, religion. So much hatred for yourself. It creates toxicity for all. It burns the entire planet. You may think all the forest fires, the earthquakes, the so-called natural disasters that take many lives are just random acts of anger from Mother Earth. No, it isn't. It is all the anger and toxicity that millions, if not billions, have created on a collective level that has resulted in this way. It is time for each one of you to start taking responsibility. The day humans learn this, is the day planet Earth can stop being a volatile place.

Stage 8: Receiving With Absolute Clarity

When you can see what I can see, the truth of your contribution to the planet, you can begin to realise that all it matters is love and forgiveness. All else is futile.

Life comes with an expiry date. It ends very soon before you know it. Do what you have got to do today, for your greater good, for the collective good, for the higher good of all. So, that when life flashes your story before you leave the body, you say, *'I'm proud of me'*.

'Live with so much compassion,

Live with forgiveness,

Live with gratitude,

That, when life flashes your story before you leave the body,

You smile and say, "I'm proud of me".'

It is your choice whether you want to go with regret or with a content smile.

The feeling of safety or security is not outside of you. No material, no amount of money, no external condition can give you that. Only when you have connected with yourself and live from within, when you are living your magic, that's when you become fearless. That's when you are truly safe. That's when you feel at home.

'Feels good to be home.
The feeling of safety lies within,
The feeling of stability,
It's all within, not without.'

Until I started on a path of awakening, I did not realise that I was lost.

You must be lost first, to be found. **Being lost means wanting to become one with the true self, wanting to go in that direction, but not knowing how and where to go.**
The soul is guiding you and when you start listening to that inner guidance, it doesn't take long to find your way back.
The true self is your home, you started from there. One day or the other, you have to find your way back there. **When you are one with the true self, you are home.** When you are home, you are truly happy, you begin to heal, you feel safe and stable because it is absolute. You must spend time in solitude to reconnect with the true self, to hear the soul's voice and to do it happily. Because you know, in that solitude you can find yourself, you can

Stage 8: Receiving With Absolute Clarity

create your magic. You know that all safety, all security lie within you, not outside of you. That's when you say, it feels good to be home.

'My Union And My Duality'
'I was weak, I was needy.
I wanted to be strong, I wanted to be independent.
I am strong, I am independent.'

This poem was written when I realised that I was jumping in and out of two realities. This realisation dawned on me only when I started to see with clarity. Sometimes I was back to the weak and needy fool, other times my strong and secure self. That is why it was written in two tenses within a stanza.

Spoken in the past, when I was a fool. Not knowing that everything I desired already existed within me…'*I was weak, I was needy'*. Spoken in the present tense… *'I am strong, I am independent.'*…affirming to myself that I am free, I am joy, I am cheerful, I am hopeful, I am found, I am pure, I am love, I am calm.

The one who affirms is the one in union with the soul. The one who was lost and weak was the fool. This is the duality, referring to the two realities, one being the soul, the True Self that is within and the other being the external self that I had acquired, the Acquired Self. Many people identify themselves with who they have become on the outside, telling themselves... *'I am weak', 'I am stuck', 'I am sad', 'I am suffering', 'I am lonely'*...none of them are true.

I began to see the duality only when I was in union. When I became one with the true self, I found that I am already what I wanted to be. I am a pure channel of divine light, divine love. I am love. I am light.

All the love, all the strength, all the calm you want to be, is already within you.

'I was lonely, I was overwhelmed.
I wanted to be love, I wanted to be calm.
I am love, I am calm.
I jump in and out between my union and my duality; and that's fine.
I have been transitioning from being naïve to mastery.'

It is alright to jump in and out between your union and your duality while you are going through your

Stage 8: Receiving With Absolute Clarity

transformation. It is part of that process. You must experience it to transition from naivety to mastery. **Because it is only in this contradiction can you see,** *'what is'* **and** *'what is not'*.

Many people live their lives in control, not in trust. They try to control every aspect of their lives, not letting go of their pain, focusing on the past, worrying about the future.

I could not trust and therefore I could not surrender. I wanted everything to be in the order that I had planned. Nothing worked out as I had planned and in that I had created a lot of resistance in my own flow of life. I had to go through much pain to learn this valuable lesson.

I learnt *'The Art Of Surrender'* through pain.

Surrender is about trusting what you cannot see. It is about trusting in the knowing that you have the power to create whatever you want even when you do not see it. It is about trusting that help is there, that someone is there to carry the heavy weights for you, but you must put them down for another to carry them for you. Many people say that they are heavy with problems in their lives and they want to be light. However, they refuse to let them go. That's what control is, refusing to put down your heavy weights. **Surrender is about letting go of that control.** It is about trusting that all is taken care of, that the Universe is always helping you. Surrender and let the Universe carry your heavy weights for you…and when you cannot trust, remind yourself… *'how do I breathe? Do I trust that air is always there for me?'*

It is an innate trust, even without your thinking. When you took your first breath, you surrendered to that inner knowing that oxygen is there for you and you inhaled it in with complete trust. If you can trust in something so precious that is vital for your physical existence, without seeing, then, what are life's challenges compared to that? Your problems that you think are so big, so important, are only nano-miniscule dots for the Universe. Learn to put them down. Allow the Universe to carry them for you.

Do you know that life force energy flows through you? Whether you are aware or not, it keeps flowing to you and through you all the time, without which you cannot be

Stage 8: Receiving With Absolute Clarity

alive. How do all these things happen without your knowing? Isn't it trust?

'Did you say, "I will not come through my mother because I do not trust the process"?

Did you say, "I do not trust there's air so I will not breathe", before taking your first breath?

Did you say, "I will not eat because I do not know how to", before swallowing your first morsel of food?'

Trust that everything is working out by design. The same way as you trust a seed when you plant it in the ground, that one day it is going to flower and bear fruits, at the right time. That's what trusting the process is all about. **Trust and surrender. That's the secret to travelling light, that's when you begin to release the past, that's when you begin to heal and grow.**

'Life Is In Surrender
Not in control'

When you trust and surrender, your life begins to flow and unfold in magical ways. When you surrender, you allow life to take you wherever you want to go. In restraint, you keep yourself in places, in situations, in relationships, in jobs that you do not really want to be in, keeping yourself in pain. When you surrender, you let go of doubt. When you surrender, you see that life is in attraction, it is just the way the Universe works. You attract as you are. You are joyful, you attract more joyfulness. You are miserable, you attract more misery. It is simple. When you know this, all you have to do is tweak your own vibration and the entire world around you changes. In repulsion, you keep yourself in a battle and never come out of it.

When you surrender, you continue to expand as life unfolds for you. You are meant to grow continuously. Most people start to contract at an early age. As they grow older, as the body goes into suffering, the trust begins to wane and the possibility of a surrender becomes smaller and smaller. You are meant to continue to expand your consciousness your entire physical life, for numerous lifetimes and never stop. That's who you are. **True living is in expansion.**

Stage 8: Receiving With Absolute Clarity

Growth is by design. You are meant to grow, grow and continue to grow, physically, mentally, emotionally and spiritually. **By design, you have the ability to expand and flourish, to become the creators of your own lives.**

When you do not grow, you become stagnant and stagnation means agony. It means being trapped in your own confinement. You can learn to allow, you can learn to surrender, to heal your past and grow, for, if you remain in the past you cannot grow. All you need is the desire to grow, all you need is to allow and life takes you there, life gives you the lessons you need to grow, nothing can stop you… *'The Power Of Growth'.*

'The power of growth, it breaks through barriers
The power of growth, nothing can stop you
The power of growth, nothing can keep you down'

'Rumble's Jenna'

The story of Rumble and Russ is a metaphor to show that one must pay attention to where one is focussing. To be aware, which aspect of your life are you adding more energy to.

That's how energy works...wherever you focus, it grows. The more attention you give, it gains momentum and becomes matter over a period. Everything is energy, your thoughts, your emotions, all of them.

In this story, Rumble focussed all his energy on the dying plant. So, he neglected the rest of his garden. He was complaining, *"why is this happening?"* He forgot that it was his garden in totality that gave him joy, not just one plant. In a short span of time, he destroyed his entire garden just because of one dying plant. In that, he killed his joy and the will to live.

'He lost the will to live,
couldn't think of planting another garden,
dreaded the loss again.

He lost the joy in his life,
lost the spark of his existence.

Stage 8: Receiving With Absolute Clarity

He lost his life.'

This is what happens to most humans. When something goes wrong in their lives, they put all their focus on the wrong. *'What am I doing wrong?'* Or *'why me, why is this happening to me?'* Or react with anger or frustration or resentment or sorrow. What one doesn't realise is that, when one does that, one is only destroying oneself. Because when you do that, you are adding more energy to the *'wrong'* thing that you do not want, by thinking about it, worrying about it or reacting to it all the time. Ultimately, you lose the joy in your life and you have nothing to look forward to, you have nothing to live for, you lose life itself.

Many people stay is grief for years and years, after they have lost somebody, either through physical or emotional separation, not knowing that they are creating more grief for themselves. Rumble represents that side of you.

On the contrary, Russ followed his inner knowing that life was not just about one matter. Losing somebody or something is part of life. He learnt to let go and focussed on all the other things that were going well. He learnt that everything fell away when they no longer served. He did not add any energy to the pain of losing, no matter how precious the plant was. Instead, he focussed on the joy that his garden was, as a whole. Hence, he created more joy for himself. He was grateful for the good things, appreciated everything…for the dying and the living. He believed that this was all part of the process and he trusted it.

Everyone goes through pain and struggles. It is how you react to your pain, that determines the life after.

'Both had a plant each that was diseased,
the same symptoms,
the same feelings.'

When people are in pain, most forget that there are so many other things that are going right. When you learn to focus on the good things, that energy gains momentum and you start to receive more things to feel good about. Just one of the clever ways of the Universe…what you give out, you receive.

Your energy is your vibration. You are a vibrational being emitting frequencies, transmitting messages all the

Stage 8: Receiving With Absolute Clarity

time. When you deeply know this and become mindful where you are focussing your attention, you can realise that, by design, you are a creator. You have the power to create the life you desire. You can receive everything you want when you learn to let go of a loss or a suffering, just the same way as Russ got *'Jenna'* back. Your life can continue to flourish. **No matter how much pain you are going through, if you learn to ignore it for a while, not add any energy to it and focus on something good, watch the magic happen.** Watch your pain disappear very quickly. Russ represents that side of you.

'He learnt that he can cherish the memories,
that everything falls away when they no longer serve.
He learnt to focus on what he's got,
to appreciate what he has,
to be grateful for everything, for the dying and the growing.

He learnt to trust the process,
to love the entirety of creation.'

Until you discover within yourself, you do not truly know how much potential you are, how creative you are. Until you make that journey within, you do not know how deep you are, how much knowledge you have in there. Until you reach out to the guidance that is available for you, you do not know how much help you have. **Until you connect with the Universe, you do not know how abundant you are, what grace you are, what love you are…** '*So Much, You Know Not*'.

'There is so much love,
You know not.'

Stage 8: Receiving With Absolute Clarity

You are an abundant being, you have all the knowledge, all the guidance, all the love that you need, it's all in there within you. You do not know it until you go in there.

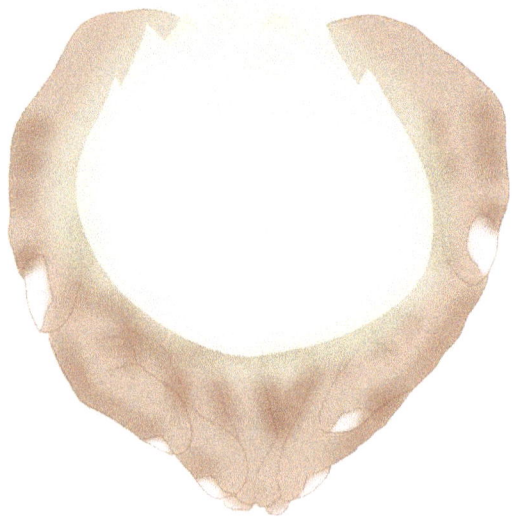

Stage 9: Becoming A Powerful Creator

Stage 9: Becoming A Powerful Creator

I Am No Longer

I am no longer afraid of suffering,
For, I am a spirit, I am well.
Suffering is only giving way to enlightenment.

I am no longer afraid of fear,
For, I am a spirit, I am strong.
Fear is only giving way to courage.

I am no longer afraid of sorrow,
For, I am a spirit, I am joy.
Sorrow is only giving way to ecstasy.

I am no longer afraid of chaos,
For, I am a spirit, I am calm.
Chaos is only giving way to serenity.

I am no longer afraid of death,
For, I am a spirit, I am eternal.
Death is only giving way to new birth.

Stage 9: Becoming A Powerful Creator

I Am A Powerful Creator

I had big dreams, I wanted to move away from where
I was planted,
I achieved every single goal I wanted,
I was an achiever,
I just didn't know I was,
For, I was a fool.

I was a powerful creator.
I just didn't know I was.
For, I was a fool.

I had big pains, I felt sorry for myself,
I moaned and groaned,
I received more pain,
It was my own doing,
I just didn't know it was,
For, I was a fool.

Words Through A Soul

I was a powerful healer.
I just didn't know I was.
For, I was a fool.

I have big desires, and it's all done.
Whatever I want, the moment I want it, it's created.
I receive with joy, I receive with gratitude,
I receive with love.
It was always so easy,
What a fool I was!

Now I know, I can create anything I wish.
If it exists in my mind, it exists in my reality.
I am a powerful creator.

Stage 9: Becoming A Powerful Creator

Dance With The Universe

I no longer am in control.
I no longer know what is happening.
I no longer know how it's unravelling.

All I know is, a miracle I live.
All I know is, a magical journey I am on.
All I know is, a marvel of a creation I am.

I am flowing, true joy flows through me.
I am blissful, divine love touches every part of me.
I am ecstatic, in this dance, I have with the Universe.

Come join me in this ecstasy.
Come join me in this bliss.
Come join me in this rapture.

Come join me in this intoxication with the Universe.
Come join me in this union with the Universe.
Come join me in this dance with the Universe.

[19] *Art Title: Dance With The Universe*

Stage 9

Becoming A Powerful Creator

When I became one with the spirit that I am, I learnt to disconnect from the painful physical body and connect with the well-being that already existed within me because the soul is always well.

'I am no longer afraid of suffering,
For, I am a spirit, I am well.
Suffering is only giving way to enlightenment.'

When you become one with the true self, and speak through the soul, you are no longer afraid. You see everything in the light that it is. No pain holds any space in your heart anymore, for, you know that it is only giving way to enlightenment. When you live from the soul that you are, you know that you are truly safe, hence, you have no fear. When you know this, you can begin to see that fear is only giving way to courage. As a spirit you feel only joy, because it is a natural state of being for the soul. Sorrow is only held on by the physical human, but it is necessary to go through sorrow in order to experience ecstasy. When you become one with the true self, the soul, sorrow only gives way to ecstasy. You no longer feel any chaos because as a spirit, you are calm, serenity is your nature. **No death exists within you, for, you know that you never die as a spirit, as a soul.**

'I am no longer afraid of death,
For, I am a spirit, I am eternal.
Death is only giving way to new birth.'

That's when you say, *'I Am No Longer'* just a physical body, I am joy, I am courage, I am ecstasy, I am serenity and I have given birth to myself.

Stage 9: Becoming A Powerful Creator

'I Am A Powerful Creator'
'I had big dreams, I wanted to move away from where
I was planted,
I achieved every single goal I wanted,
I was an achiever,
I just didn't know I was,
For, I was a fool.'

Only when you become a powerful creator can you see that you have been a fool. You can receive everything you want, because that is just how it works in this wonderful Universe we live in. You ask through your desires and when you ask, you are given.

I didn't know I could create everything I wanted. So, I created by default. I moaned and groaned in pain, I didn't know that by doing so, I was creating more pain for myself. I didn't know I had the ability to heal myself.

Now I know, whatever I want, I can have it. Whatever dreams I have, the desire to share true knowledge, to help others, to be of service to myself and to humanity, to play a part in the human spiritual evolution, they are all done, they are all created. I create knowingly now.

You are a powerful creator simply by design. You are a powerful being, here to create your own reality.

'Now I know, I can create anything I wish.
If it exists in my mind, it exists in my reality.
I am a powerful creator.'

After I completely surrendered to the Universe, I gave up all control. I no longer asked anymore, what was happening or how it was going to happen. I began to completely trust and, in that, life manifested into a miracle. Everything started to flow abundantly through me, to me and for me…pure love, true joy, infinite guidance, divine healing, absolute peace…and in this connection with the Universe, I started to dance in ecstasy, in bliss, in complete rapture.

Stage 9: Becoming A Powerful Creator

When you know that you are a marvel of creation, when you know that you are a spirit on a magical journey, you become one with the divine that you are. You know that you are a fragment of the Source light, the same light that created the Universe.

When you are one with the Universe, you '*Dance With The Universe*'. That's when you want to share your love, your joy, your bliss with everyone, you want to intoxicate everyone with your ecstasy, with the wish, '**may everyone feel this way**'.

'Come join me in this ecstasy.
Come join me in this bliss.
Come join me in this rapture.

Come join me in this intoxication with the Universe.
Come join me in this union with the Universe.
Come join me in this dance with the Universe.'

This is the story of my transition. From a fool to awakening, from darkness to light, from ignorance to knowledge, from naivety to mastery. A fool's journey that everyone goes through, knowingly or unknowingly.

A Thank You Prayer

There is so much knowledge out there for everyone. If you feel you are not receiving it, it only means that you are keeping yourself in a limited space and not allowing yourself to expand. Only you are limiting yourself from infinite possibilities, no one else.

I remember many a time, I cried, *'when is it ever going to end?'* The pain was so vast for me to take. But now, I see it all. The unfoldment is beautiful. I had to go through pain, experience many aspects of humanness, to truly know what life is all about. It was my pain that gave birth to my journey inward, to become aware, to receive true insight, to ask, to receive, to allow, to heal and grow.

So, I thank all the pain and suffering, I thank all the challenges. Because they come for a reason, to give us life's valuable lessons that we would have never known or learnt, so, thank you, thank you, thank you.

A Thank You Prayer

Thank you, Universe, for everything.

Thank you, Divine Mother, Divine Father.

Thank you, my Angels, Spirit Guides, all Masters and Teachers, all Healers and Helpers, all Gods and Goddesses, all Light Beings, all Energy Beings, thank you all.

Thank you, Mother Earth, for this beautiful place, that we live in, that we call home.

Thank you, Mother Nature, for the beautiful creation, the wonderful trees, flowers, plants, birds and bees, insects and animals. Thank you all for playing a part in this beautiful system that we have. Thank you for your contribution. Thank you for sharing your joy. Thank you for sharing your beauty. Thank you for sharing your love. Thank you for playing your part, thank you.

Thank you, Air, for being there at all times. So that, we may breathe in pure oxygen to fill our body and our brain. Air for all living beings, nourishing all plants, feeding all plants and animals and the entire Universe. Thank you.

Thank you, Water, for cleansing and purifying us, and healing us, feeding us, nourishing us, nurturing us, giving us life force, for, without water we cannot survive. Thank you, Water, thank you, thank you.

Thank you, Divine Fire, for cleansing us, for purifying us. Divine Fire has the power to cleanse and burn away any challenges, any pain, any suffering. Surrender to the Divine White Fire. Invite the Divine White Fire, to cleanse, to burn away any pain and suffering, any challenge. So, thank you Divine White Fire for cleansing, for purifying and for healing. Thank you.

Thank you for all the beautiful Food that nourishes and nurtures our body. Thank you, Mother Earth, for providing this beautiful food. Thank you.

Thank you for the wonderful Life. That every day we get to practice all kinds of experiences…whether it's joyfulness, sadness, gratefulness, hopefulness, wonderfulness. All kinds of emotions that we get to experience, every single day. So, thank you, thank you life.

A Thank You Prayer

Thank you, Life Force Energy, that is flowing through us and to us, at all times. Without which, we cannot survive, we cannot be a living being. So, thank you life force energy, thank you, thank you, thank you.

Thank you, my Body, for working every day, giving me eyes to see, giving me a mouth to speak, allowing me to enjoy and hold with love, with my arms and my legs for walking me around so that I can see places. Thank you for the space around me, thank you.

Thank you, my Organs for always being there, doing your work, thank my heart for pumping, thank my stomach for absorbing and digesting all my foods, thank you. Thank you, my liver, my kidneys, thank all my organs, thank you, thank you for doing your work all the time, thank you.

Thank all my Family and Friends, Acquaintances and even those people, that I may not know, but still serving me, somehow helping me and showing me, sometimes those people may not even be the nicest, even they are serving a purpose, showing me what I need to see. For, everybody in our lives are mirrors, the good, the bad, all of them. When the good comes, it's only showing you the work that you have done on yourself. And when the bad shows up as well, the mirror is showing you, this is what you need to work upon. Life is a mirror. So, thank you for this beautiful and clever system that the Universe has, that creation has, that nature has, thank you.

Thank you for every Day. Thank you for every Night, that we get to relax our body, rest and repair.

Thank you for the beautiful day. Thank you for the Sun, thank you for the Moon, thank you for the Stars, thank you.

Thank you. Thank you for all Living Beings. Thank you. Thank you, there is so much to be grateful for every single day, there is so much to be grateful for, thank you, thank you, thank you.

Index Of Focus

Preface

Pain acts as a catalyst for us to break through who we have become to get to who we truly are.

Introduction

Only when one awakens can one see what a fool one has been.

Everyone's journey is the same, which is, walking from the outside to the inside. The only differences are the experiences we go through while walking this distance.

Stage 1: Being A Fool

That what she thought was love, was only attachment.

Stage 2: Pain

Pain is the much-needed darkness. It is the key that unlocks the door to allow light in.

One cannot jump from total darkness to light in an instance.

Letting go makes space for new experiences to come in.

Stage 3: Solitude

Life must continue to change just the way seasons do.

Solitude is required for inner work.

Solitude is choosing to quiet the mind.

In solitude, you start to hear the whispers of the soul.

The thing about expectation is that it is an energy where you have given your power away to another.

When you love because you are love, you have no expectations.

You remain complete.

Stage 4: Awakening

the Acquired Self, the Human (the one that had become) and the True Self, the Soul (the one that is).

The realisation is important because without it you can never make the move.

You must not allow a wrong turn to keep you in the wrong place for your entire life.

The sooner you realise it, the quicker you learn to grow and heal.

You are an *'Energy Being'* in a temporary vehicle called the human body.

You are never alone.
but perfection is knowing that challenges are perfect for your journey.
Because that is the journey everyone has to do, travel from the outside to the inside. For, only when you find the true self do you find true peace, true love, true joy.
Freedom means taking responsibility for yourself.
Who you are is guided by the soul, you must learn to listen to the whispers.
What you are, is not about becoming something on the outside, it is about allowing yourself to shed the outer layers of what you are not.
You must go on the journey, for, you have growing to do, learnings to carry forward.
Letting go is freeing.
When you choose, you are willing, you are allowing life to lead you, to become who you really are.
You are a complete package as you are.
When you feel the love within, you see that *'There Is Beauty Everywhere'* because you see through the eyes of love, the eyes of Source.

She is the Divine Mother who loves and nurtures all beings.

When you learn to truly become one with nature, you learn the true essence of your own life, every life, every existence. You are nature.

Stage 5: Reflections; In And Out Of Duality

There are lessons everywhere.

But it is when you stop blaming others and start taking responsibility for yourself that you begin to see, that it is you who created that wrong.

'I did this' is a powerful realisation for transformation.

It is the realisation that is important.

Pure love is always in the present.

Because love is not about another, it is within you, it is everywhere, it is always here and now.

But it is important to keep the trust that you are a work in progress and that everything is in process, even when you do not see it.

It takes time to unveil what is hidden underneath so many layers of lies.

In those struggles, in the name of sorrow, insecurity, fear, all they seek is love.

You lead by example, not by control.

Only when you know from within can you teach another.

It is time to wake up.

Many humans numb themselves with unnatural things they consume by labelling them as *'food'*, *'drinks'*, *'medicine'* and *'happiness'*.

In order to evolve, it is important to become aware that you are living in an upside-down world, that your system is outdated.

All those days are wasted days because you are only adding more to your suffering, to your darkness and keeping yourself further away from the light.

You are all born pure and divine.

Hence, that, what you think is a mistake in life, a wrong in life, has a value.

Everything is happening exactly as it is needed for your journey.

The more aware you become, the better you get in learning from your mistakes and grow.

Stage 6: Coming to the light, Becoming A Spirit

When you learn to watch it, that's when you start to wake up. When you start to wake up, you begin to live your true reality.

The longing to come out of the darkness is required to build the strength to emerge.

Each one of you is a seed.

You have within you, all the guidance to flourish. You must allow the seed within you to grow into the abundant being that you are.

you get exactly what you need in order to unlock your treasures.

No matter what you are going through, no one's pain is greater or smaller. No pain is better or worse. Everyone goes through exactly what they need to go through in order to learn, in order to grow.

There is only one purpose for everyone, that is to find who you really are.

As long as you keep going, no matter how challenging it seems, you can get there one day.

The only thing that you take as a spirit is the soul's learning and that is what you carry forward. What you have started today can never be lost.

It is only when you learn to truly free yourself, can your society, your country, your planet become free from suffering.

It starts with you. Be the free spirit that you are to free humankind.

Stage 7: The Beginning Of Divine Guidance

All you have to do is pull out the weeds from your mind. But it is when you innerstand and practice the true meaning of love, gratitude and forgiveness that you really learn to clean yourself out.

Comfort keeps you in the same state.

It is now time to rise to that light.

It is time to move into this space of inspiration and become the creators that you are, the love and light that you are, the unity consciousness that you are.

It must come from the purity of love that you are.

When women on this planet begin to activate this wisdom and embody their true light, that is when an exponential shift can happen in human evolution.

Stage 8: Receiving With Absolute Clarity
You are born fully loaded with every information you need for your existence.
The absence of a quality highlights the value it had in your life.
When you do everything from a place of knowing, nothing is random, all is crystal clear.
Love is an energy that heals all pain and transmutes all fear.
When you learn how to heal, you know exactly what is happening, you are grounded in your present and you have no worries about your future because you know that you have got it.
Love because you are love.
When you are connected to the true energy of love that you are, that's the knowledge you carry forward through time, that's when you see everybody and everything with love, that's when you do everything from a place of love.

One heart is a powerful transmitter of this beautiful sequence.

One heart has all the love to heal the entire planet.

When you start to be that one, the light spreads.

Compassion is about forgiving those who may have hurt you, knowing that the reason why they hurt others is only because of their own wound which stems from ignorance. So, they couldn't have known any better. In that knowing, you forgive them.

Compassion is not about your feelings for another. It is about being. Be compassion. Be love.

One has to go through darkness to give birth to the desire to be the light. One has to go through the pain of being stuck to want to fly.

But you must have patience, you must learn to trust, which, in itself, is another lesson.

That's when you become *'The Energy Being'* that you are. Every vibration you emit as an energy being, contributes to the collective energy of the planet.

When you can see what I can see, the truth of your contribution to the planet, you can begin to realise that all it matters is love and forgiveness. All else is futile.

It is your choice whether you want to go with regret or with a content smile.

Being lost means wanting to become one with the true self, wanting to go in that direction, but not knowing how and where to go.

The true self is your home, you started from there.

When you are one with the true self, you are home.

All the love, all the strength, all the calm you want to be, is already within you.

Because it is only in this contradiction can you see, *'what is'* and *'what is not'*.

Surrender is about trusting what you cannot see.

Surrender is about letting go of that control.

Trust that everything is working out by design.

Trust and surrender. That's the secret to travelling light, that's when you begin to release the past, that's when you begin to heal and grow.

When you trust and surrender, your life begins to flow and unfold in magical ways.

When you surrender, you continue to expand as life unfolds for you.

True living is in expansion.

Growth is by design.

By design, you have the ability to expand and flourish, to become the creators of your own lives.

That's how energy works…wherever you focus, it grows.

Everyone goes through pain and struggles. It is how you react to your pain, that determines the life after.

No matter how much pain you are going through, if you learn to ignore it for a while, not add any energy to it and focus on something good, watch the magic happen.

Until you connect with the Universe, you do not know how abundant you are, what grace you are, what love you are.

You are an abundant being, you have all the knowledge, all the guidance, all the love that you need, it's all in there within you.

Stage 9: Becoming A Powerful Creator

No death exists within you, for, you know that you never die as a spirit, as a soul.

Only when you become a powerful creator can you see that you have been a fool.

Index Of Focus

You are a powerful creator simply by design. You are a powerful being, here to create your own reality.

When you know that you are a marvel of creation, when you know that you are a spirit on a magical journey, you become one with the divine that you are. You know that you are a fragment of the Source light, the same light that created the Universe.

'may everyone feel this way'.

Acknowledgements

In the non-physical realm, I offer infinite gratitude to The Source of all knowledge, the true limitless intelligence, the source of all creation. I give thanks to the Divine Mother for your love, for your nurture, for your healing and for all creation. I give thanks to the Divine Father for your love, for your protection and providing me with everything that I need and more. I thank all my guides, all light beings and the entire collective energy of the Universe who have played a part in my journey.

Thank you all for your boundless love, wisdom, infinite guidance, divine healing, abundance of everything, for being with me at all times and for everything that you have taught me. I knew nothing and you poured everything into me without any limitations. For that, I am eternally grateful and feel the abundant energies of the Universe through me, to me and for me all the time.

Most of all, I thank you for initiating me into my role.

Acknowledgements

In the physical realm, I give thanks to Vittorio Mattioli for a wonderfully constructive report which helped me tremendously in structuring my book, to Eileen Flynn for a fantastic editing job on my manuscript, to The Susan Mears and Merlin Literary Agency, to Susan Mears and Janet Lee Chapman for a brilliant reader's report that helped instil the confidence that I am on the right path.

Big thanks to Sumer Paul for helping me in every possible way while I was going through my journey of writing this book. Truly appreciate it.

Deep gratitude to my human mother for bringing me into this physical world, for taking care of me while I was young and loving me till her last breath in this avatar. I thank my human father who shared so much love despite the short time in the physical experience. I thank all my bloodline…brothers and sisters-in-law, my sister and brother-in-law, my nieces and nephews; my friends, my tribe, my soul sisters and brothers, my soul community and everybody who have played a part in my evolution story, knowingly or unknowingly.

Finally, I thank you, dear Reader for connecting with me through this book.

I thank you all.

About The Author

Rajya is a guide, a mentor, a teacher, a mystic and an artist. She is a receiver and a transmitter of divine messages, to help guide the spiritual evolution of humankind. Born in Manipur, India, she is now based in the United Kingdom. She has been on her conscious journey of self-discovery and self-healing for almost 15 years.

Through her physical, mental and emotional challenges, she learnt that pain is the key that unlocks our true potential and started on a journey of unravelling…tapping into her own power within, finding her true self, creating a life that she had always wanted, living a life of passion. In the process, reinventing and rejuvenating herself. Empowered by her experience, it is now her desire to inspire others become their best selves, to awaken to their true light, so that they can go through the journey of life with knowing and ease.

You can connect with her on www.rajyalovelife.com

A Special Dedication

The poem, *'Ho Ima! All I Wanted Was Love'* (in Stage 5) is a special dedication to my mother, *'Ima'* and my brother, *'Tamocha'*, in their loving memories, who are no longer in these physical avatars.

Blessings From Goddess Tara

[20] *Art Title: Green Tara ~ A New Earth Is Here*

Prints of the titled illustrations in this book are available on:

www.rajyalovelife.com

www.ingramcontent.com/pod-product-compliance
Lightning Source LLC
Chambersburg PA
CBHW042123100526
44587CB00026B/4168